Moravian Mafia

Religious Greed and Dictatorship

Samuel Nathan

iUniverse, Inc.
NEW YORK   BLOOMINGTON

Moravian Mafia
Religious Greed and Dictatorship

iUniverse books may be ordered through booksellers or by contacting:

iUniverse
1663 Liberty Drive
Bloomington, IN 47403
www.iuniverse.com
1-800-Authors (1-800-288-4677)

Because of the dynamic nature of the Internet, any Web addresses or links contained in this book may have changed since publication and may no longer be valid.

ISBN: 978-1-4401-5868-1 (sc)
ISBN: 978-1-4401-5867-4 (dj)
ISBN: 978-1-4401-5869-8 (ebk)

Printed in the United States of America

iUniverse rev. date: 7/24/2009

CONTENTS

INITIAL THOUGHTS.

There are those who would claim that this work is inspired by God or that the spirit moved the act of writing it.

The author says that this book was inspired by his perception of the often false and potentially exploitative design that notions of that type are frequently pronounced and embedded in the concept of 'God's-inspiration'; especially when the real motive of whatever subject, is really a desire for universal acceptance.

As a trained analyst (systems); it becomes second nature for this author to see through most of what could be classified as 'bogus claims' based on the fanciful theory of divinely induced guidance.

How many times we hear about ministers of the cloth, professing that God told them this or God told them that, usually after the event, whatever it was.

Although this work is the reaction to a particular Moravian church, it is clear that collections of generalities, pervasive within the Christian faith exists and is leant on heavily by ministers of the cloth, especially when ad-libbing under pressures of the sermon or other occasions when pontificators are doing their act.

The mafia notion is borrowed from its standard reference to some Sicilian 'tight-knit' family, labelled as outrageously brutal in methods adopted to obtain solutions deemed to be in the best interests of that family, regardless of whatever necessary actions were, even to points that included individuals killing others, on occasions employing unsavoury techniques.

While the author does not know of an instance where any connecting satellite or affiliated organization of the subject Moravian church has committed or encouraged physical murders; it is argued that instances exist where acts against the spirit would merit such a similarity. Since the church in focus is supposed to provide spiritual guidance, upliftment and benefits; deliberate or thoughtless acts in that area, especially designs to elicit material advantages because of spiritual blackmail say, could be just as damaging. Certainly, the organization that operates under the Moravian banner in the region appears to sew seeds of greed in those pastors representatives sent to this country and the subject church in particular, a trait strongly evident in those of Antiguan descent than other nationals. They have certainly managed to murder the Moravian ideals, held sacred to many conservative and older followers of the faith

This author professes to be not very good at behaving as a second class citizen in any societal setting, even whilst himself a foreigner in other countries around the globe. Thus, he does not take kindly to outsiders who come here with the notion that nationals of this country are in any way inferior to them. He does not mind equality but objects most vehemently to being of lower class status than any visiting professional, even if they reach these shores disguised as ministers of the cloth. When any clergical individual is attached to a church, that person is initially given the courtesy to the dignity of his station, together with all the respects that he or she should be given by virtue of the position within the church and in our case, that dispensation is initially given without question. It is indeed a thin line for that person to maintain the supply of respects given in recognition of the embedded status and confusing the nature of any well meaning congregation with docility. Once that misunderstanding creeps into the relationship, it is then an easy step to jump to the position of making unreasonable demands. When initially, the overgenerous congregation, in its willingness to welcome the new minister and aid the settling in process, fails to correct the minister's exploitative attempts; that notion of docility could be seen by the minister as re-enforcement. Therefore attached ministers must take care to demonstrate clearly that the good nature of his host congregation is not exploited, abused or turned into a tool with which to make outrageous demands on the initially generous congregation. That individual has to take care not to transmit airs of superiority, contempt or apply to his or her person, any other demeaning attitude. Indeed, the minister sent to serve a congregation is supposed to do just that: serve the congregation he or she is attached to; not seek to manipulate it to service his or her personal needs and/or desires. Such notions are exploitative and unbefitting any person claiming to be a messenger from God.

Using God's name by any minister to extract artefacts, services, material things or worldly goods of any kind for the minister's personal convenience, consumption, control or use has to be despicable by any right thinking person. That practice removes the focus from ministering to spiritual needs and puts the minister in between those to be exploited and spiritual contact with God. "Paying for God's work!" is a popular phrase; when the real meaning is for the minister to coax more funds out of the pockets from unsuspecting believers.

CHAPTER ONE,
A HISTORICAL VIEW!

The church of Moravia, not formally labelled as such, because it first surfaced in Germany, would be a fitting description of how the movement we know today as Moravianism began life. It is interesting to note that the movement incubation period was conceived from dissatisfaction with established church practices of that era, during the mid fifteenth century. A time when the Catholic Church had strict controls over their version of the faith, which in fact was the only one permitted and heavily policed to preserve its hold on matters relative to Christianity, not very much different from what obtains now within the Moravian hierarchy, clinging to outdated practices of deceit and misguidance!

Jan Hus was considered to be a heretic by the Catholics of his day. Initially a Roman Catholic priest, he was excommunicated and later burned at the stake for practicing influences absorbed from John Wycliffe. Jan's ideas encouraged the formation of the Hussites and Taborites or the Bohemian Brethren. It was that group which gave life to the Moravian Church among exiles from Moravia resident in Germany. The main thrust for the Moravian way of approach to worshiping the Lord then, was their dissatisfaction with the degree of deviation by Roman Catholic practices from those of biblical teachings.

In effect they were a bunch of idealists, verging towards perfection as they saw and understood the written word. In passing, it is mentioned here, that John Wesley, credited with being the founder of Methodists was influenced by the teachings of Jan Hus and that observation should give some idea how pervasive his influence was. It is ironic that the discrepancies which influenced the Taborites to break with Roman Catholicism and eventually cost Hus his life, has come full circle, is evident within the subject church and perhaps others of the faith also (more on that later).

There is little doubt in my mind that if it was possible, Jan considered to be the founder of the Moravian movement, would turn in his grave if he could see what these boys from Antigua have done and is doing to the manifestation of his ideas. He would undoubtedly ask himself, was it worth losing his life, for this modern day mafia to exploit and in the process, turn his ideals into vehicles for their personal ease and comfort?

Towards the mid-eighteenth century, cells from the movement which long left its original base found its way to islands in Caribbean waters, during the epoch when Negroes were regarded as property rather than persons. Cell members belonged to the same Caucasian race as were the slave trappers and traders. The slaves were black Africans; unlike their cousins from the north of that continent, who were lighter of skin, straighter of hair and Arabic of race classification. The unsuspecting black Africans, having been trapped like animals, reduced to life-styles below that of wild animals. They were stripped of humanity, locked in confining conditions by fellow Africans and Arabs before being shipped out from their own land, still in dehumanized conditions and in spaces that animals were given more consideration about, before reaching, among other destinations, shores dotted around the Caribbean Sea.

The passage across the Atlantic Ocean, from east to west in vessels provided according to the technology of that period was perpetually confining, cramped and grossly disgusting. The spirit of human eagerness to hold on to life, regardless of levels of depravity to which it sink is one of the facts of existence that still marvels humans enjoying comfortable circumstances today. Although many captives did find the necessary internal fortitude to cope with fluctuating bad circumstances of their particular voyage from Africa to the Americas; some did find ways to escape their long traumatic ordeal: either intentionally or otherwise. However, most did make it to other lands thanks to their inner and physical strengths.

When those early unwitting settlers got to these islands, their initial start to life on new homelands, although less cramped than on ship experiences, continued to find life discomforting, unpleasant and bewildering. On top of that, thoughts of future existence would have been futile if and when they did occur because the human animal would have been reduced mentally, spiritually and emotionally to zombified displays of life.

Regardless of race or creed, anybody who had to endure an Atlantic crossing in the bowels of a wooden barge with sails on, for weeks, sometimes months would have been reduced to some state displaying all or more of the negative attributes that affected those early slaves, arriving on the islands, after any such voyage.

Once on land again after any crossing, the next form of depravity would be suggested by the auction block to decide who got to be the new owner of the person locked inside of the stolen body before it was transformed, driven to behave like a robot or humanized machine. Once bought, the continuing bewildered individual had no hope of employing meaning to his or her existence. The clever ones' best hope would have been to try and learn the rules of their new found life, whatever it turned out to be.

The bubbling dynamics of any island community confronting those early Moravian missionaries would have included a mix of: slave ships' arrivals, human captives at varying stages of acclimatization and some who would know no other land but that which contained them. Buying and selling the black person, extra to the auction block, would have been normal and even more vibrant than trading in livestock.

The hardened whites of the islands went about what was for them, their normal businesses, living off the backs of the oppressed blacks, without thinking about whatever hardships their privileged existence caused to beings they considered as lower than animal life, especially in families that owned pets. Their range of desires; taken without question, from the already oppressed black persons and certainly without care or thought. That was the mindset of the day; it would have been misplaced if the then ruling elite found time to consider or display what is now considered to be ideas akin to humanity.

The above picture would have been a typical dynamic, present in any from the myriad of islands that spoke English, Danish, French or Spanish and produced sugar.

Thus when the Moravian missionaries reached the islands of the west, their introduction would have been to an atmosphere flavoured according to the peculiar mix of varied souls inhabiting them. As newcomers to the scene; it is fairly certain that those early missionaries did not leap into acts of demanding that existing white overlords start treating their black bondsmen and women fairly or even reasonably and it is doubtful that in the fullness of time, they ever did express such concerns.

History, with its generous intent to flavour those bygone missionaries as men of God, who arrived in these islands with the zest to bring relief to the downtrodden slaves as their primary goals, ascribe such intentions to early Moravians arriving on these tropical islands. However, examinations of their 'pre, current and post' Caribbean experiences, customs and norms suggest to this author motives which may not have been what traditional and kind historians claim.

The Moravians in their country of origin were accustomed to living with and around their own kind of white people. In those far off lands, locked within some distant corner of Europe; if they heard about black people at all, it would have been in the form of distant, unconnected or remoter tales. First hand experiences with Negroes were highly unlikely. Therefore the possibility of them leaping through such a void to compassionate concerns for the black man on remote islands would have a high probability against it.

It has already been remarked that these missionaries were fanatical men, who inherited their faith from men who rebelled against the teachings of the Roman Catholic Church, possibly because the then standard church was becoming too liberal for their tastes. They, the rebels, broke away because they understood, interpreted and tried to practice stricter interpretations from their bible.

Those who write about historical Caribbean life and effects on slavery tend to behave like ostriches, especially when Christianity is part of the equation. However, the first, and most obvious, thing religion ducks is that there is no specific condemnation of slavery to be found anywhere in the Bible. At no point does God express even mild disapproval of enslaving human beings, robbing them of what freedom and independence they might previously had. On the contrary, the Bible depicts God as both approving of and regulating slavery, ensuring that the traffic and ownership of human beings proceed in an acceptable manner. In many cases, the regulations display a horrible disregard for the lives and dignity of enslaved individuals, hardly the sort of thing one would expect from a loving God.

Passages referencing and condoning slavery are common in the Old Testament. In one place, it states:

"When a slave owner strikes a male or female slave with a rod and the slave dies immediately, the owner shall be punished but if the slave survives a day or two, there is no punishment; for the slave is the owner's property. (Exodus, 21:20-21).

In other words, the immediate killing of a slave is punishable but a man may so grievously injure a slave that they die a few days later from their wounds, **without** facing any punishment or retribution, even though the latter could be more horrible than immediate killing. All societies in the Middle East at that time condoned slavery; therefore, it should not be surprising to find approval for it in this document. Indeed, by Middle East standards, the above would be commendable - after all, there was nothing quite so advanced anywhere else in that part of the known world. However, as the will of an all-loving God, condoning possible torture towards a slow death was abominable.

As a side note, the King James Version of the Bible presents the above verse in an altered form, replacing the word "slave" with "servant" - thus gravely misleading Christians as to the intentions and desires of God's will. One more reason to reject fundamentalist claims that the King James Version of the Bible is the only true and valid translation!

The New Testament, unfortunately, is little better than the old. Jesus never even came close to expressing disapproval of the enslaving of other human beings and many statements attributed to him reveal a tacit acceptance or even approval of that inhuman institution. Throughout the Gospels, there are passages like:

A disciple is not above the teacher, nor a slave above the master (Matt. 10:24)

Who then is the faithful and wise slave, whom his master has put in charge of his household, to give the other slaves their allowance of food at the proper time? Blessed is that slave whom his master will find at work when he arrives (Matt. 24:45-46).

Although Jesus is using slavery in order to illustrate larger points, the question remains: why he would directly acknowledge the existence of slavery without saying anything negative about it.

The letters (rightly or wrongly) attributed to Paul are even worse, making it clear that the existence of slavery is not only acceptable, but that slaves themselves should not presume to take the idea of freedom and equality preached by Jesus too far by attempting to escape their forced servitude.

Let all who are under the yoke of slavery regard their masters as worthy of all honor, so that the name of God and His teachings may not be blasphemed. Those who have believing masters must not be disrespectful to them on the ground that they are members of the church; rather they must serve them all the more, since those who benefit by their service are believers and beloved. Teach and urge these duties. Whoever teaches otherwise and does not agree with the sound words of our Lord Jesus Christ and the teaching that is in accordance with godliness, is conceited, understanding nothing, and has a morbid craving for controversy and for disputes about words. From these come envy, dissension, slander, base suspicions, and wrangling among those who are depraved in mind and bereft of the truth, imagining that godliness is a means of gain (1 Tim. 6:1-5).

Slaves, obey your earthly masters with fear and trembling, in singleness of heart, as you obey Christ; not only while being watched, and in order to please them, but as slaves of Christ, doing the will of God from the heart (Eph. 6:5-6).

Tell slaves to be submissive to their masters and to give satisfaction in every respect; they are not to talk back, not to pilfer but to show complete and perfect fidelity, so that in everything they may be an ornament to the doctrine of God our Savior. (Titus 2:9-10).

Slaves, accept the authority of your masters with all deference, not only those who are kind and gentle, also those who are harsh. For it is a credit to you if being aware of God, you endure pain while suffering unjustly. If you endure pain when beaten for doing wrong, what credit is that? But, if you endure when you do right and suffer for it, you have God's approval. (1Pet. 2:18-29).

What is to be made of passages such as those already quoted? It must be concluded that the author(s) did not disapprove of the institution of slavery and probably regarded it as an appropriate part of society. Again, slavery was common in all contemporary societies, and it would be surprising to find condemnation in them. If those authors were indeed divinely inspired, as is commonly thought, then we must conclude that God's attitude towards slavery was not particularly negative. Christians were certainly not prohibited from owning slaves, and anyone who did not agree was directly condemned. There was no conflict between being a Christian and being an owner of other human beings.

No "common sense" interpretation can deny such things without doing violence to the text itself, and nothing can be criticized as being 'taken out of context'. Even if it is considered that the Bible was written in a primitive, barbaric age and is representative of prevailing attitudes; those were undoubtedly the influences that strict biblical scholars read and lived by, as early missionaries to the Caribbean were.

How did the early Christians deal with the issue of slavery? There was almost universal approval of slavery among church leaders. Christians vigorously defended slavery (along with other forms of extreme social stratification). Attitudes were: slavery was instituted by God and an integral part of the natural order of men. At all points, their reasoning was clearly and easily supported by the Bible passages quoted.

In their own words, they say:

The slave should be resigned to his lot, in obeying his master he is obeying God ... (Saint John Chrysostom).

... slavery is now penal in character and planned by that law which commands the preservation of the natural order and forbids disturbance. (Saint Augustine).

These attitudes continued throughout European history, even as the institution of slavery evolved and in most cases, slaves became "serfs" - little better than actual slaves and living in deplorable situations, which the church declared as divinely ordered.

Not even after serfdom disappeared and full-fledged slavery once again reared its ugly head was it generally condemned by Christian leaders.

Edmund Gibson, Anglican Bishop in London made it clear in the 18th century that Christianity freed us from the slavery of sin; not from earthly and physical slavery. The freedom which Christianity gives, is a freedom from the bondage of sin and Satan, from the dominion of men's lusts, passions and inordinate desires; as to their outward condition; whatever that was before, whether bond or free, their being baptized, and becoming Christians, makes no manner of change in it.

The first ships bearing slaves for the Americas appeared in the early seventeenth century, initiating over two centuries of human bondage in that part of the globe; bondage, which would eventually be called a "peculiar institution." That institution always received theological support from various religious leaders, both on pulpits and in classrooms. For example, through the late 1700's, Reverend William Graham was rector and principle instructor at the Liberty Hall Academy, now Washington and Lee University in Lexington, Virginia. Every year, he lectured the senior graduating class on the value of slavery and used the Bible in his defense of it. For Graham and many like him, Christianity was not a tool for changing politics or social policy, but instead to bring the message of salvation to everyone, regardless what their status of freedom were. Those attitudes were certainly supported by biblical text.

As Kenneth Stamp wrote in The Peculiar Institution, Christianity actually became a way to add value to slaves in America:

… when southern clergy became ardent defenders of slavery, the master class could look upon organized religion as an ally … the gospel, instead of becoming a means of creating trouble and strife, was really the best instrument to preserve peace and good conduct among the Negroes. It is suspected, that was also true for Caribbean clergy mentality.

Through teaching slaves the message of the Bible, they could be encouraged to bear the earthly burden in exchange for heavenly rewards later on - and they could be frightened into believing that disobedience to earthly masters would be perceived by God as disobedience to Him. Ironically, enforced illiteracy prevented slaves from reading the Bible themselves. This was ironic because a similar situation existed in Europe during the Middle Ages, as illiterate peasants and serfs were prevented from reading the Bible in their own language - a situation, which was instrumental in the Protestant revolution. Now, Protestants were doing much the same thing to African slaves: using the authority of their Bible and the dogma of their religion to repress a group of people without even allowing them to read the basis of authority on their own.

The same knock on effect being practiced by modern day Moravian clergy: the high degree of secrecy, their closed attitude to what goes on within the higher echelons of the Moravian management strata and the prevalent laziness among congregations. It is a state, which leaves those unwilling or unable to think for themselves, at mercies of enterprising and unscrupulous ministers with greed and dubious ambitions as major motivating forces.

In time, as northerners decried slavery and called for its abolition, southern political and religious leaders found an easy ally for their pro-slavery cause in the Bible and Christian history. In 1856 Reverend Thomas Stringfellow, a Baptist minister from Culpepper County in Virginia, put the pro-slavery Christian message succinctly in his *"A Scriptural View of Slavery:"*

" ...Jesus Christ recognized this institution as one that was lawful among men, and regulated its relative duties ... I affirm then, first (and no man denies) that Jesus Christ has not abolished slavery by a prohibitory command; and second, I affirm, he has introduced no new moral principle, which can work to its destruction ... "

Of course, Christians in the north disagreed - and some denominations, like Quakers, appeared not to have been afflicted by slavery. Interestingly, most abolitionist attacks were pinned to the premise that the nature of Hebrew slavery differed in significant ways from the nature of slavery in the Americas. Although it was meant to argue that the western form of slavery did not enjoy biblical support; it nevertheless tacitly **admitted** that the institution of slavery did, in principle, have divine sanction and approval so long as conducted in an appropriate manner.

Reasons why it was easy to discriminate and enslave blacks included biblical and Christian support based on the earlier institution of slavery itself. That discrimination and the choice to enslave blacks only, was made primarily on the basis of what has become known as the "sin of Ham" or "the curse of Canaan." Occasionally there would also be defenses for the practice of ascribing inferiority to blacks by asserting that they bore the "mark of Canaan."

Genesis, chapter nine, relates that Noah's son Ham came upon him sleeping off a drinking binge and saw his father naked. Instead of covering him, he ran and told his brothers, Shem and Japheth. The "good" brothers, returned to cover their father. In retaliation for Ham's 'sinful act' of seeing his father in the nude, Noah puts a curse on his grandson (Ham's son), Canaan? Cursed be Canaan; lowest of slaves shall he be to his brothers" (Gen 9:25).

Over time, the interpretation of this curse was that Ham literally was "burnt" and that all his descendants had black skins, marking them as slaves with a convenient color-coded label for subservience. When and how the idea gained widespread acceptance is questionable but anti-slavery, religious and political leaders worked to refute it for a long time, for over a century they tried.

Today, biblical scholars note that the ancient Hebrew word "Ham" does not have to be translated as "burnt" or "black" - but there is unfortunately little consensus on how the name and passage **should** be interpreted. Further complications came from positions of some Afro-centrists: that Ham, although not actually cursed (despite what the Bible says!) was indeed black, as were many other characters in the Bible. Once again, people end up reading the passage as supporting their own racial assumptions.

Although many Christians today would be horrified at using the Bible as support for racism, they should recognize its use in just such a fashion by Christians in America and the Caribbean. With similar justifications that Christians today use the Bible in their defense for their favourite ideas.

The cultural and personal assumptions of the early missionaries and pro-slavery biblical authors, quoted so far are probably obvious to us now, but it is doubtful that they were obvious to white missionaries in their time. Similarly today, few people are aware of the cultural and personal baggage they bring to their beliefs and readings. Globally, people assume the truth of what they believe, are determined to find divine sanction for those beliefs in whatever holy books they read, be it the Bible, Koran or the Karma-Sutra.

Throughout history, the idea that an individual interpretation is, just "common sense" was used, on every side of every issue, including the topic of slavery and the early attitudes of white missionaries to it.

Just like it was when the Conquistadores were accompanied by so called priests, as the soldiers walked through the killing zone, massacring Amerindians; each time any soldier killed a native; the nearest priest shouted at the most recent murderer, "You are absolved my son!" Waving a cross in the face of the latest killer.

It is not suggested that Caribbean missionaries of the Moravian faith behaved as blatantly as preachers seconded to the Conquistadores. However, their early days on these islands slotted into a timeframe when they had to seek approval from hardened white islanders who were long standing members of that society. If the early missionaries did not pay homage to the embedded seniority of the local whites, they would not have been allowed to function in any way, shape or form, certainly not without increased resistance or outright sabotage; it was as simple as that. The new arrivals initially had to satisfy and appease the ruling elite, with convincing assurances that they, the missionaries, would not upset the status quo. They had to work their way into what ever system existed at the time and that required socializing, seeking to strike friendship pacts and generally live in good harmony with the already resident whites, all of which meant that their opening gambits included making sounds and gestures that pleased the hardened slave owners and manipulators. In other words, they had to exhibit stances of support for the white masters, including displaying superiority where blacks were concerned.

During that era, black people were not welcomed or allowed to participate in church worship in any of the main churches operating on these islands. Apart from the belief that God only listened when white people spoke to him; keeping blacks outside church doors when occupants were members of the master race, got support from ministers and parsons of all denominations. They in turn found justification from biblical passages that suited their purpose, including the following passage: Deuteronomy, Chapter 23, Verse 2, reads: "One of illegitimate birth shall not enter the assembly of the Lord; even to the tenth generation none of his descendants shall enter the assembly of the Lord."

When preachers of the day explained the ramifications of that biblical text, already hardened attitudes became even more rigid and white racists clung to that piece of scripture as if, it was carved in stone. Some even subjected it to memory and when those initial Moravians sought support for commencement of their projects, the more vocal biblical students quizzed the missionaries indirectly about their intentions and ideas with regard to the type of membership they aimed to attract. The more cleaver of the missionary group acted wisely, spoke as abstractly as were managed and answered along lines that suggested. "We are here to serve the Lord our God according to the ethos manifested by the five basic ideals that our church holds dear, strives to weave into the fabric of our existence and service in the name of Our Lord and Saviour Jesus Christ."

When asked about those ideals, missionaries answered the following: The first in the list would be '*Simplicity*'; it is a focus on the essentials of faith and a lack of interest in the niceties of doctrinal definition. They would quote Zinzendorf's remark that the Apostles say: "We believe we have salvation through the grace of Jesus Christ. ... If I can teach any man that catechism, it will make him a divinity scholar for all time!" (C. H. Shawe, 1977, p 9). From this simplicity flows, secondary qualities of genuineness and practicality.

The second ideal is *Happiness,* which is the natural and spontaneous response to God's free and gracious gift of salvation. There is a difference between a genuine Pietist and a genuine Moravian. The Pietist has his sin in the foreground and looks at the wounds of Jesus; the Moravian has the wounds in the forefront and looks from them upon his sin. The Pietist in his timidity is comforted by the wounds; the Moravian in his happiness is shamed by his sin' (C. H. Shawe, 1977, p 13).

Unintrusiveness is based on the Moravian belief that God positively wills the existence of a variety of churches to cater for different spiritual needs. There is no need to win converts from other churches. The source of Christian unity is not legal form but everyone's heart-relationship with the Saviour.

That ideal attracted questions about perceptions of converting slaves to the Moravian faith. To which missionaries, 'still boxing clever', extended the idea that God already gave them their own faith and would not expect they, the Moravians to interfere with God's work in that way. Answers implying that the intent to upset the status quo in any way was not in their plan. They learned their diplomacy from earlier experiences at Savannah, Georgia in the southern United States

Another ideal: *Fellowship* is based on this heart-relationship. 'This Moravian ideal has been to gather together kindred hearts ... Where there are "Christian hearts in love united", there fellowship is possible in spite of differences arising from intellect, intelligence, thought, opinion, taste and outlook. ... Fellowship [in Zinzendorf's time] meant not only a bridging of theological differences but also of social differences; the artisan and aristocrat were brought together as brothers and sat as equal members on the same committee' (C. H. Shawe 1977,pp 21,22).

Responses to such an idea included: "I hope that you all aint going to bring negroes into your church and expect white people to go around shaking their hands, when you talk about bringing aristocrat with artisan together! This island, do not want ideas of that sort in it!"

Once more, the missionaries would have to deny any such plans and in a sense, deny the possibility of introducing that aspect of their Moravian ethos.

Finally, *the ideal of service* entails happily having the attitude of a servant. This shows itself, partly in faithful service of various roles within congregations but more importantly in service of the word 'by the extension of the Kingdom of God'. Historically, this has been evident in educational and especially missionary work. Shawe remarks that none 'could give themselves more freely to the spread of the gospel than those original Moravian emigrants who, by settling in Herrnhut [on Zinzendorf's estate], how they gained release from suppression and persecution' (p 26).

It would appear that in the interval between the formation of Herrnhut and Moravian missionaries arriving in the Caribbean, some twenty years went past and in that span of time, the initial fervour was heavily diluted, a lot of it diminished already. Considering the set back experienced at Savannah, Georgia in the southern state of North America, where a group of missionaries landed in 1735. In the face of a very intense form of slavery practiced by hardened white supremacists. That cell of Moravian missionaries had to vacate that society with extreme haste because those ideals claimed to be their driving force were, ruled out of order. They were incompatible with the ethos of that white supreme community. Standards of the southern whites could not exist alongside those professed by the Moravian missionaries. The white ruling group gave the missionaries no physical or emotional space to operate in; the missionaries in turn, to ease their level of discomfort, left that state of Georgia with indecent speed, never to return. It took them another five years to regroup their bearings, found themselves in New York and more civilized communities to the north of the continent. To this day, Moravian churches predominate, mainly in northern states because the early attempts of the missionaries found more cozy and acceptable conditions in those areas where the intensity of slavery were mild or non-existent. The society of New York and other civilized states were easier to cope with and gave the missionaries breathing spaces to re-motivate themselves, recover sufficiently their supply of zeal and again, experiment with intense slave communities.

Thus when those early missionaries arrived in the West Indies, New York was an easy launching pad and they were sufficiently armed with an ample supply of 'don'ts'. They learnt lessons from Savannah about clever ways to deal with entrenched racists who were almost, always on the lookout for outsiders who would compromise their grips on the islands. Also at that time, there were established contacts between slave owners on Caribbean islands and those of rigid slavery states on the north continent. Word already reached the islands about the Moravian experience in the slave state of Georgia and the first arrivers to the Caribbean got wind of that fact. Therefore, in the interests of survival, it made good sense to adopt a very low profile when it came to advertising that the Moravians planned to bring salvation to the downtrodden of the islands, if indeed that was any part of their plan. Additionally, although the Caribbean whites felt secure in their superior status, each community was restricted and could not develop the sort of quick response in terms of instant physical support from likeminded neighbours as their American cousins could summon. The Caribbean islands separated by water as they are; whereas on the American mainland, one plantation only had to raise an alarm and the whole state would rush to the call, wherever it came from. Therefore, within the island geography and mentality the more whites who showed support and joined their numbers added to their sense of security, even if those new comers were men of the cloth.

When the Moravian missionaries of New York recovered from their bad experiences after Georgia, did their assessment of life outside Europe, across the Atlantic and took lessons from previous mistakes. They revaluated their early ideals and adjusted accordingly until they felt ready to get back into the 'fray'.

New arrivals from the mother congregation in Europe had to be acclimatized by the experienced, hardened veterans and locally recruited 'wanna-be-Moravians'. The emerging dynamics created in the process, a completely different set of missionaries, with revised orientation as their purpose and objectives. Considerations that encouraged questions with regard to historical claims that those early missionaries journeyed to the Caribbean, primarily to take salvation relief to the black slaves, easing the burdens they bore then.

Another area of speculation has to be concerned with the fact that within the slave industry, when those Moravian missionaries sailed to the islands, transportation of human cargo from Africa to the Caribbean was still flourishing. It became known as the second leg of a well-known then and now famous 'triangular run'.

The first leg of the triangle, referred to the initial part, where slave ships left Bristol, England and sailed to the west coast of Africa, the Gold Coast it was then and today, known as Ghana. On a typical voyage, ships carried trinkets used as bait that would encourage slave hunters to trap unsuspecting Africans, who within their own context, went about the business of their culture, without considering or entertaining the slightest notion that fellow human beings were in business to trap and rob them of existences they took for granted. When caught, they were shocked and devastated. Having been trapped, individuals became items of the human stock, herded into corals on the Atlantic coast at Fort Almena or similar holding dungeons and kept shackled until slave ships arrived to take them into completely different worlds beyond their comprehension, conditions of which have already been described earlier in this work. Journeys from Africa to any port in the Americas were different strands of the second leg, comprising the triangle. Delivery of their human cargo complete; those same initial slave ships became conveyers of differing produce back to England, thereby completing the third leg and the triangle. Those boats, filled to capacity with sugar, cotton, tobacco and different products loaded at ports where slaves were most recently off loaded.

A significant and pertinent consideration which over-kind historians failed to take into account about early Moravian missionaries of the era was:- If as claimed, the missionaries aim was to bring relief to suffering negroes: Why did they not go to the western shores of Africa, at points where the second leg of the 'triangular run' commenced? Locations like Fort Almena, where for days on end, new slaves existed until the next inhumane contraption called a ship arrived. Those poor souls, shackled, kept alive on starvation morsels and herded into confined spaces or in the open, had to dispose of bodily waste, ate and breathed in environments that were perpetually oppressive. Repeatedly, day after day, for however long it took the next vessel to arrive. Each new day brought with it increasing numbers of live bodies, struggling against the chains that held them in line to share confined limited spaces. Why did the missionaries not go there in the first place?

That would have been an ideal point to make their influence felt. From there, they would have had access to the ears and minds of those ungodly types who daily went in search of unsuspecting persons made in the image of God but dark skinned. Those hunters mercilessly trapped individuals who had no reason to believe that they were about to be taken away from: their homes, their friends, the life styles weaned into and never to see loved ones ever again.

Surely to catch the perpetrators at source where their evil commenced would have been a worthy goal! Logically, that is where the work of delivering salvation would have been most effective! Thereby, providing more good and better service to humanity than intervening after so much harm and damage were already done. Intervention at that early stage for each shipment would have been much more impressive than waiting until after those souls were, against their wills, removed from whatever culture they knew. Suffering at Fort Almena and similar reception depots, would have eased, lives wasted at that same fort and others like it, in time. Plus, losses where desperate young people jumped off ships, still wearing shackles as they tried to get back to homes remembered but having no idea about the vastness of the ocean and its absorbing power, they jumped to certain death in desperation and after shock. Then there were those, brutally used then disposed of from vessels where human life had minimal value. The shear wastage of humanity during those long sea voyages, across the Atlantic might not have been, if only those missionaries went to West Africa to practice their craft; instead of going west to the Americas, where pioneering work was already established. Instead of waiting until the blight on human existence got to the state where it was when claims of salvage testified to good works on their behalf!

Indeed, it was not until the late nineteenth century that Moravian missionaries went to Africa, Tanzania and the Congo. Comments about locations and timing are wasteful exercises, since by that time, slave ships trading in human cargo was no longer current. The point of sending missionaries to Africa later, probably was somewhat akin to the real reason for sending them out at earlier times, to the Americas, what it always were: delivering salvation for church policy reasons.

Although claims that initial aims of the Moravian church and their mission to Caribbean islands, included notions that their 'burning desire to take the gospel of Jesus Christ to all oppressed people and help to ease their burdens' are debatable and suspect. There is little doubt that Moravian preachers eventually provided beneficial effects in helping to bridge the wide gap that existed between slaves and masters. Even though legal innovations added to circumstances that gave rise to latent desires on parts of those who found inevitable changes difficult to digest. For a start, the Moravians were first in allowing slaves to congregate outside their church while the whites enjoyed comforts of sitting inside. At least they did not continue to shoo blacks away from listening to the word of God in close proximity to church buildings. Then one day, when the intensity of falling rain encouraged one brave and enterprising young woman to throw caution to the wind and leave it outside; braved whatever the taboo was and went inside the church to shelter, then others followed suit. When the pastor failed to object to that intrusion, none of his white congregation did either, thereby creating a half-hearted sort of precedent. Alas, that incident did not create scope for repeat inside visits when days were nice and sunny. It took a lot of 'chasing outs' of black people from inside churches before ushers got fed up and with encouragement from kind hearted ministers, the practice of chasing slaves out from inside church got less diligent.

Since the advent of human creation, people have always been attracted to gatherings of other people. That is to say, the collection of human beings, have a tendency to pull others to it. That explains why in earlier times, black slaves grew attracted to gatherings of white people inside churches. On the islands, when whites began praising the Lord God in buildings named churches, black people were encouraged to keep away from those odd but attractive looking structures, with large and colourful glass windows. However, those acts of discouragement added to initial curiosities and attractions of what went on inside churches grew; increasing already heightened desires to learn meanings of perceived actions, performed by the white folks, as they acted out rituals that gatherings in churches did. Another fact of inquisitiveness is that the longer onlookers are kept at distances from perceived attractive acts; is the more tempting those scenes become. That abstract snippet of psychology is one clue as to how religion caught the imagination of slaves on estates and villages: seeing the white folks behave in their peculiar fashion, encouraged slaves themselves to scramble together aspects of their own cultures. They were psychologically ready for the leap to embrace what went on inside those churches reserved for whites only, because initially they could not enter those aloof clubs. Much the same reasoning applies to why it was that big houses readily found extra hands to help with serving at functions. They presented opportunities to be amongst attractive looking gatherings. The net effect of mounting interest in religious antics was that gradually slaves forced their way by sheer will, into the religious life white folks appeared to treasure so dearly and went to great lengths to keep it to themselves. Attitudes of Moravian clergymen were among the first to undergo gradual change, reacting to slave numbers, which grew in proportion to white residents and as the number of available churches increased. When newly opened churches entered the 'market place' of white souls, distribution got thinner among the newly established ones, to the disadvantage of churches displaying tolerance and understanding towards the black man's social plight. Softer missions rapidly lost attention from white congregations, compared to the more rigid houses of God.

A useful indicator here has to be, the fact that it was over seventy-five years after Moravian missionaries arrived in the Caribbean that slavery officially ended in the region. Why was that? Why did it take so long to bring that inhumane practice to its end? If it was that their initial objective was to ease the suffering of their fellow man who were slaves. The answer has to be: they the missionaries, at best, were ineffective and why was that? The tempting answer would be that they got lost in their own agendas: rather than focusing on black souls; they used convenient ones: those whites who were willing and able, to freely offer theirs!

Thus, the dynamics of population growth and racial balance began to make their presence felt. The situation was that Roman Catholic

Churches, traditionally catered for persons of Irish and Portuguese extractions attracted, a portion of the hardened whites from churches that grew softer towards blacks. However, the main flood were to the Anglican persuasion because that faith was seen as most loyal to the mother country and even though rumours of anti-slavery rumblings filtered through from England, the belief was that it would never work. None of the hardened slave owners believed that Great Britain would stand for anything, which would damage the earning potential from its colonies and the result of that notion was they transferred beliefs to serving God into the Anglican style.

Empty pews inside Moravian churches to clergymen were depressing sights, especially when there were numerous persons begging for entrance. Thus, as whites left the Moravian rows, blacks easily filled them up. It took pastors awhile to get used to the kaleidoscopic effects but time healed that for towards the twilight period of slavery, Moravian churches got to be churches for black people in the Caribbean. Not because it was the original plan of those early Moravian missionaries; more to do with desires and lust of black people for something that the white man had, treated as sacred in denying access to it by the slaves. It was sheer determination by those blacks to get something that white people had, they wanted, eventually got and that was in spite of the fact that Deuteronomy, Chapter Twenty-Three, Verse 2, forbad the black man from entering any congregation of the Lord, since none of them were married biblically. Nor did it end there for afterwards the same 'cat and mouse' congregational game followed the other initially, inaccessible churches, causing the perpetual ebb and flow of bodies between churches that is still going on to this day, as new churches rise up and others disappear.

Analysis certainly suggest that when those early Moravians arrived on these Caribbean islands; they had their own agendas, which had little to do with the claim that they came with burning desires to bring the Gospel of Jesus Christ to oppressed people on these shores or that genuine concern motivated them to come here. On the contrary, they came to build their own brand of religious practice and used what they found to be most convenient. Yes, at certain points, they provided a sort of education but that was a means to an end. If they were going to work with black people, then it was necessary to teach that audience to follow their customs, that could only happen if the new congregation knew how to behave and because reading was a necessary tool for that exercise; black people who could not read had to be taught, if they were to be effective congregations. Had those missionaries not taught the dedicated blacks how to read; then diminishing congregations were going to be their unattractive alternatives. They would have to pack up and go back from whence they came, because Sunday and other services had potential to be boring. Therefore, it is true to say that, the early Moravians were instrumental in the development of slaves and their descendants. However, even if those missionaries did not come, development of black people would not have suffered and analysis, also suggests that black people's development within the region, covered by historic involvements of Moravians missionaries got to where they are, more by thanks to their own efforts and initiatives than what historians like to credit missionaries for! Look at those islands where there is no Moravian church! They too are at the same stage of advancement as countries, which hosted the early missionaries!

CHAPTER TWO,
MORAVIAN IDEALS.

The ideals of Moravianism are principles suggested by codes traditionalists developed over time and outlined in an account of ethos on the Moravian Church, given by one of its British Bishops, C H Shawe. He gave a series of lectures at the Moravian Theological Seminary in Bethlehem, Pennsylvania. There he described the Spirit of the Moravian Church as having five characteristics: *simplicity, happiness, unintrusiveness, fellowship and the ideal of service.*

THE IDEAL OF SIMPLICITY.

Simplicity, interpreted as living in uncomplicated modes and resisting the temptations that manifest themselves in various forms, especially in today's world where technology is changing so very rapidly, providing attractive options, almost daily. Such temptations can be irresistible to the weak minded and they are not free. Inventors and suppliers of cell phones or flat screen television sets do not send them to the minister's manse with instructions to sample these new gadgets on the house. Everything has cost and has to be paid for, either in monetary value or in kind. Even prepared meals that 'once upon a time' used to appear at the front or kitchen door of the manse as donations from well meaning church members. Such generous gifts are not now as varied or frequent as they once were. That vanishing practice is a reflection of how life styles have evolved, enforced through changing but increasingly tense styles of existing. The necessity of keeping up with the demanding pressures with which ordinary people have to cope, forces the pull away from the simple life. Such pressures promote into mounting importance values of speed, wealth, popularity and sexuality. However, according to the teachings of Jesus, in God's kingdom, those values should be slow, simple, humble and chaste.

Increasingly as individuals are diverted, away from expectations that were simplistic in nature, towards more elaborate hopes, desires, dreams and yearnings. Aspirations that once were not ostentatious grew outrageously into costs and they in turn create wants that are expensive in monetary terms. Such drives create pressures that cause ordinary people to yearn for riches or more realistically, they begin to wish for riches. Nor do desires for unreachables stop at being just longings for 'out of reach materials. Frequently, they begin to imitate life styles that are out of their reach. Desires by ordinary people for more wealth than they currently own have grown exponentially and such ambitions, apart from taking their owners into problem areas with creditors and draws their owners into conflict with the teachings of Jesus Christ. According to the Gospel of Luke (12:16), Jesus explains how the rich man, because he is rich, can use his wealth to amass more wealth. However, he is foolish to be spending his time and energy in this way, says Jesus, for it diverts him from spiritual life. This theme recurs throughout the Bible: wealth is an obstacle to the spiritual life.

Once the concept of simplicity in serving God gets out of sight, all sorts of confusing and conflicting distractions begin to get in the way, qualities that suggest conflict of the desire to appear Christian begins muddying the waters. The speed of trying to keep up with the pace with which modern life pulls, causes the slow, deliberate gait that gives perspective and enables one to see relevance to areas that undue haste or speed would otherwise cause one to miss in the blur which increases with speed. The hurry to replace tried and tested methods with unproven experiments and desires to make them work regardless of unexpected consequences. Anticipated desirous outcomes coupled with speed to arrive at some new state of operation that results from tampering with what is already there can eventually do more harm than good and in terms of serving God, may indeed be counter productive; in much the same way that throwing the baby away with the bath water after washing it.

One facet the concept of progress throws at society is the continuous and frequent appearance of new churches. Every new church that enters the marketplaces where Moravian churches operate adds to pressures that existing churches already in the environment experiences. How are Moravian churches supposed to respond to that dynamic? The missionaries of old, when faced with similar dilemmas, reacted by teaching and intensified Moravian values under a banner of pride and identity; it is now fashionable for this new batch of pastors to copy and attempt to absorb the substances, styles, behaviour and greed of their new rivals. Such responses thoughtlessly abandon concepts of Moravian valued qualities for whatever the competition appears to be offering. Of course that type of appeasement with abandon, carries with it a price and it would appear the cost, more often than not, tends to be values that makes Moravian what it was and should continue to be but is in imminent danger of being lost.

Among the casualties usually, is the slow approach to serving God. Serving the Almighty gets replaced with speedier styles because these new organizations calling themselves churches, competing for members, become models to be emulated by so-called modern day Moravian churches. Thus, instead of maintaining the dignity and traditions, developed over centuries, Moravians, more than other developed churches with long historical pedigrees, take on the fast moving new comers in contests, commercially known as competition. In the process abandoning values, standards and other unique qualities with which the layperson or members with Moravian traditions used to identify with. Desires of speed then become pre-eminent as far as the new movers are concerned. It is usually the modern and predominantly Antiguan pastor who occupies the driving seat in moves to evangelicize Moravian churches, steering them along merry but misguided paths when they enter into arenas where the competition for bodies who want to serve God is taking place.

In a typical situation, he the pastor, the ordained man of God, the man invested and trusted with the ideals of Moravianism is one and the same who sells out and plunges his responsibility headlong into the fray, competing against other churches with questionable aims, ethics, ethos and intent! Can it be that Moravian pastors do not learn about values peculiar to the faith anymore, or is the doctrine still officially supported but the quality of ministers available for Moravian work is so poor that the moment they are assigned a ministry, their training 'goes out of the window', is forgotten or discarded? Are they misguidedly supported, from within the ranks of higher echelons who then fail to provide adequate supervision in ways that are supposed to maintain Moravian qualities? Whatever the answer is, it results in a 'fast-lane' approach to serving God, using methods far removed from the Moravian way.

Speed in service to God also has degrading side effects, making ministers hungrier for desires of the material world, more than is decent or befitting to their calling. So that when their continuums of speed react with those of greed, they find themselves pushed into climbing, higher along greed dimensions, to points where they perpetually look at possessions of their congregation and what they have. One Moravian minister of past acquaintance regularly asked from the pulpit for any member to clear his overdraft. Then they begin to make oblique demanding noises in sermons, using God's name indecently that are tantamount to blaspheming in the things they say that God wants us to do.

An important message from New Testament teachings states clearly that Christians are to seek God's Kingdom, for there is where our salvation and happiness lie, it entails among other things, living a modest life. Riches will lead us away from God and true well-being. The virtue of simplicity is necessary for accomplishing those goals and is a main feature of the Christian lifestyle. God knows that the clerical structure of Moravian clergy, from bishops, right down the line to installed pastors, have either forgotten or chose to ignore that message, if they ever knew about it. The imbedded blatant greed that radiates in this province is outrageous; it is so intensely absorbed, by those persons of the cloth, ruling over the Moravians Diaspora that they no longer care who sees it. The ingrown avarice is so boldly expressed that it appears to be embedded in their psyches to the point where they do not realize that their greed shows!

Once the fact of greed works its way into the consciousness, that presence manifests itself by the associate condition of 'want' as opposed to 'need'. In this province, the 'greedy wants' emerged from within the highest echelon: the bishops. About ten years ago, the bishops themselves concluded that modest lifestyles associated with the status of being exalted clergymen was much too modest for them and instantly, almost over night, spent all reserves available from the 'provincial kitty' on luxuries which bore glitz that princes would envy: plush homes, latest chuffer driven limousines, sometimes more than one. They went wild and nobody could stop them from spending, not even after the money ran out. That situation, instead of providing lessons for chaste living, only whetted their appetites and rapidly followed it up with entrenched greed. Those leaders of Moravian clergy immersed themselves into the newly discovered but rich lifestyles complete with impressions of wealth. Of course, it was wealth! Church money, that they the greedy bishops regarded as theirs to do with as they personally wished. However, to perpetuate newly found luxurious habits, they levied heavier taxes on the various constituencies that were Moravian churches in conferences, spread around the region. Suddenly field pastors had to find exorbitant quotas of funds for submission to headquarters where ravenous bishops waited to continue their spending binge at provincial base. Initially, individual ministers were flabbergasted! Alas, Moravian ministers exhibit devoted loyalties that must be a part of their indoctrination into that particular branch of the priesthood. It would not be surprising to find out that secrecy was included in their calling to serve and that their first loyalty is to the bishops or the office that they occupy. Thus, although the Lord's guidance with regards to the pitfalls of wealth may be neatly sidestepped by extravagant bishops, they cannot escape the fact that they are living the life, regardless of what Jesus taught on that subject. Although they could technically claim, not to be owners of great personal wealth, living as if they were is a technicality that may work logically, though it is certain that the good Lord will see through their wafer thin veneers.

Progress being what it is, suggests that as time galloped by: while traditional ministers who were in harness before the bishops got greedy, shook their heads from side-to-side, tut-tut ting and secretly disapproving of their bishops behaviour. Their attitudes of secrecy or perhaps fear from provincial repercussions summarily made no difference for their collective consciences failed to manifest into action that would cause the tide of greed to stop or even slow down. Indeed, the bishop's greed over time, developed into a ministerial standard or a life style for ministers of lower orders to emulate, especially those nurtured in the provincial seat. Even parsons already installed abroad, on returning home for whatever reason, once they saw the lavish lifestyles enjoyed by their overlords, vowed to implement observed lavishness back in their own attachments. Of course, in Antigua itself the 'copy cat' effect was already at work, the younger Moravian ministers there, saw the bishop's living conditions as the norm and sought to evolve their own versions. Indeed, quality of living for the senior clergy there evolved into effective advertising attractions, drawing Antigua nationals to the ministry within our regional Moravian faith. It would not be surprising to find that within the province, there are more ministers from Antigua than any other country of the group! Even islands much larger and more populous with vastly greater numbers do not produce as many Moravian ministers. Furthermore, it is highly probable that if Moravian pastors of non-Antiguan extraction were, counted together, they would be outnumbered by their Antiguan colleagues. Such is the state of the ministry for this regional Moravian ministry. Embedded greed has spread so widely, it has become an attraction in the recruitment for pastors to spread the word of God, which coincidentally, contains teaching against the very attractions, which drew them to the priesthood in the first place and that has to be contradictory!

Should the sitting minister deliberately court popularity by behaving outrageously? The 'Book of Order' for Moravian churches obliquely warns against such behaviour. There is the question about the type of behaviour can be considered as outrageous? Certainly, factors such as the pastor's character, perceived attitudes and observed antics need consideration. It does not feel right that the basic personality of any minister should not contain the quality of humbleness. Confidence yes but when an entity as diverse as a congregation encounters a minister who is perpetually over-confident, it can easily be interpreted as arrogance. When a minister mostly displays the impression that his way is the only way, giving the idea that his mind is preset and likely to be against whatever subject reaches his attention. The same stern rebuff for every item raised by a particular segment of the church, leads to the safe assumption that an overgenerous dose of conceit lurks in the shadow of his or her mind. That interpretation by discerning church members soon begin to look and feel as if the minister will not listen to the desires of his flock and is determined to perform according to his own plan, regardless of what the congregation wants. Therefore, the minister who arrives at a church with such a mindset must be considered to be working for himself instead of God or the congregation. Essentially, if the assumed 'man of God' arrives to minister, fails to conduct any kind of fact finding as to the character, needs and other factors that affect the host congregation, that minister missed a critical part of his function. Furthermore, if the same minister immediately dives into what he thinks he wants to do regardless of what his audience should get then there has to be a lot of ignorance of the conceited variety in that minister's make-up and anyone displaying such qualities cannot be described as humble or given the benefit of knowing what he is about!

According to John 13, 12 - 20, after Jesus washed the feet of his disciples, he told them, [Verse 14] " ...If I, your Lord and teacher have washed your feet, you also ought to wash one another's feet." [15] "I have given you an example that you should do as I have done to you." [17] "If you know these things, blessed are you if you do them

It is not expected that the minister would go around washing people's feet but he should certainly insert some humility into his approach and treat his flock with better respect by doing them the courtesy of investigating what needs are before deciding what he is going to do with them, even before arriving! The minister certainly should not move around, radiating airs of continuous superiority. Even if his natural disposition makes it difficult for him/her as pastor to be humble, there is an incumbent duty to try and portray an image that he can serve God humbly. Is that not, after all part of his work?

What is to be concluded about a minister, who after requesting large donations from the congregation, when one particular member was asked to donate One Thousand Dollars for a declared worthy cause; When that person called the minister to ask the title to which the cheque should be addressed; received a rebuke from the parson, "I do not work on Mondays!" It is fairly certain, that God was not angry with the near donor when she tore up the check.

What kind of example, is set by a minister who arrives over one late for Sunday service, then makes an entrance in the style of showbiz, television preachers and later proceeds to hold the congregation captive for hours after services normally terminate. Either he was experimenting with the congregation and treating it as his captive audience or forgot to prepare his sermon beforehand. Bearing in mind, that the larger segment of the congregation are elderly people, some of whom take medication with varying time constraints and at specific intervals, such behaviour is dangerous! When spoken to about the lack of concern in that kind of performance, the pastor displaying what looks like bad manners, gets entrenched, is unrepentant and says, "Nobody is going to tell me how long I must preach!"

Arrogance like that is out of place in any church and unacceptable from a resident minister. The pastoral representative of the Almighty ought to have understanding, consideration and a willingness to listen to members of his congregation. God knows, that is part of the humble quality, which any self-respecting minister of the cloth should possess!

You shall love the LORD your God with all your heart, with all your soul, and with all your mind. This is the first and great commandment. And the second is like it: You shall love your neighbour as yourself. On these two commandments hang all the Laws and the Prophets." – (Matthew 22:37-40.)

These great commandments have been re-written in action but not in words, to the edification of bishops, general overseers and pastors. (Thou shall love they, the pastors with all thy substance, intellect, wealth and health, and thou shall love their family as yourself). May the good Lord have mercy on us! Especially when we see, our Moravian ministers involve themselves in sidelines related to the love industry.

The detached observer has personal notions about what entails the definition of love. We know of the love that happens between a man and a woman. The church's attitude to the fulfillment of that kind of love is for those involved to marry by customary, traditional method and then use that union to build families. That is an adaptation of biblical references to marriage, it is what has come to be known as the root of family union and mainly initiated by that romantic love.

Another strand of the love concept has a platonic quality. It is at its best when sexuality is not involved and indulgers can freely express and openly display that type of love towards each other. Christian societies subscribe to both types of love, the first to initiate the family building blocks, the second is the type suggested by 'Unitas Fratrum', the United Brotherhood, commonly known as the Moravian Church, because the church is meant to be built around the concept of brotherly love and that is supported by Psalm 133, 1: "Behold how good and pleasant it is for brethren to dwell together in unity!.."

However, of late modern Moravian ministers appear to be going through a third phase, experimenting with the love concept, which dwells in the region of colloquially termed, local phraseology 'anti-man'. It is suggested, those in that category are there through some hormone imbalance and if that is the case then their condition is no fault of theirs. However, 'their interactions' or suggestions of it can make others not in the practice uncomfortable. As far as the bible is concerned, God destroyed Sodom and that other place because of men performing sexual acts with each other; today, men giving impressions of feminism boldly step and strut around as if they are proud of the sexuality they advertise and it appears that some ministers condone such bold displays of it. That a minister of the cloth should adopt one or two as his sons may be misrepresenting the sex but that would be his God given right. Alas, one of the characteristics of such persons is that they like to display their particular brand of airs and that is inappropriate in a church, especially when applied to with senior members of the congregation who seek to perform charitable acts to the pastor or his family, giving the impression that behaviour is inspired by their adopted father. That has to be the wrong interpretation of brotherly love!

There are communities where same sex unions are allowed. This society is not one of them where that act is officially sanctioned. However, the practice occurs privately at prestigious hotels. Since it is not legal, such ceremonies occur in private, behind the four walls of the host hotel. However, to give unions of odd couples, looks of authenticity, the establishment employs local pastors to conduct those ceremonies. It transpired that officiating at those gay functions became a lucrative sideline for resident Moravian ministers. That money-spinner became such an attraction for persons of the cloth that it caused massive friction within the Moravian ministry fraternity. The superintendent, related to one of the set who officiated at odd weddings on the side, had the controlling hand as to who got which job to marry the next couple. Another of the gay marrying Moravian ministers developed the notion that he, who is related to the superintendent, received more than his fair share of the trade and complained to her along those lines. Who told him to do that? The complainant became an outcast among the minister set. In due course, the he left the ministry because of the in-conference unfair management of 'ministering to marrying gays' plus other grievances and got a better-paid job locally. The bishops at conference headquarters quickly got in on the act and because the superintendent and relative were both Antiguans took a hand in the matter against the complainant who was not Antiguan. However, the non-Antiguan was married to another Moravian minister (a female, also not from Antigua). In double quick time, the posting of complainant's wife to serve in Tobago materialized! Now, the peculiar thing about Tobago is that non-Tobagons are not allowed to work there, even if they are married to Moravian ministers. The morale of the story is clearly, keep same sex love away from Moravian ministers or God only knows where they will end up. It has to be obvious how spiteful the bishops were and these are supposed to be men of high spiritual caliber. The way in which those Antigua ministers ganged up on the outsider is worthy of any respectable mafia operation and within their own ministry set! If they can behave like that towards members of their own ministerial club; what are they capable of against unenlightened congregations? The mind boggles!

THE IDEAL OF HAPPINESS

"For I have given you an example, that ye should do as I have done to you … If ye know these things, happy are ye if ye do them." (John 13-17.

There are many things in this world, which can bring temporary joy and happiness. Things like sufficient money, business success, good health, loving family, loyal friends, pretending to be something or someone that you are not and Moravian ministers who would rather be evangelistic fall into this category. Alas, no worldly good or pretense can bring enduring joy and happiness. It results with being content, regardless of what one has!

This ideal reflects an emotion that individuals should experience; if not before, certainly during and after Sunday services, at what stage depends on personal level of acceptance. If that is not so, there is little doubt, that place is not right according to the Moravian philosophy. Failing to experience happiness in church suggests a disconnect: that can be due to: the person experimenting with the Moravian brand of service, assuming that it is of the correct version and is not certain about their religious needs; the pastor being ineffective, doing the wrong things or himself could be in the wrong church. Increasingly, ministers forget or ignore what it is to be Moravian; in their desire to attract popularity to themselves, they forget or ignore the Moravian ideals and complicate the service, sometimes string of services. Especially those who watch evangelist television, they often think and believe that what they see on the screen is to emulate in the Moravian church, over which he or she is steward. Once that happens, the Moravian quality becomes diluted and the beginning of the rut starts. That situation then gives cause for wonder about the quality of training necessary for entry into the Moravian ministry. Questions about requirements of familiarity with Moravian doctrine, ways of conducting service under the banner of a Moravian church spring to mind. The Moravian Book of Order stipulates the character of Sunday service: P400 lists the necessary order to be followed as Hymn, Litany/Liturgy, Lesson, Canticle/Hymn, Lesson, Hymn, Sermon, Hymn, Benediction. That paragraph goes on to explain that the prescribed order be closely followed at morning services, strongly suggesting against deviation. However, there can be elasticity at the evening service. In over four years, the above, prescribed order has never been practiced in the Moravian church, which I attend regularly. Successive ministers who fancy themselves as evangelistic hotshots.

Changing the traditional order of service, either because the minister wants to experiment or through pretense to be something other than what it should be is dishonest. Firstly, Moravians who know what they want from their particular brand of service, go to Moravian churches because of the inherent ideals, learnt over time. When anyone interrupts the routine suggested by the order traditionally prescribed for church rituals then those who attend for that spiritual diet has something precious and sacred removed from expectations. What happens then is the happiness of being in church is shattered, the experience becomes uncomfortable and painful and a disconnect results. Only those affected know how deep the pain of such shock penetrates! Those religious thugs, calling themselves ministers do not know the extent of damages for which they are responsible. They most probably have no idea about the costs of their experiments, especially if Moravian ideals are lost to them. It is strongly suspected that many do not care or know about such ideals and never did.

We should be seeking to show God our love for Him in practical ways – in the reading, believing, and obeying His Word; in worshiping with others "of like precious faith"; and in "doing good unto all men, especially unto them who are of the household of faith", 2 Peter 1-1, Galatians 6-10. Not go through the motions of pretending to have concern when in reality they are only interested in pursuing selfish interests.

It is quite possible that one will become poor, fail at business, lose health, separate from a loved one, die, lose our spouse, friends or illusions. Even if we gain all of these or more during our lifetime and keep them, 'sooner or later', we must leave them all behind and "go the way of all flesh. The saying is true - 'You cannot take it with you!

It is a lesson that members of the modern Moravian ministerial set ought to pay more attention to, as already mentioned, the greed and avarice on display between them suggests that they do not take much notice, if any of that particular message.

There is certainly an aspect of existence among the minister class, which suggests that if they are not in control of abundant resources, especially that which gives personal comfort, they cannot be happy in what they do or with what they have. Honesty in normal people would indicate that if there is any truth in what is said; a change of plan, in many senses, need consideration. The principle of contentment, suggested by Count Zinzendorf when he first founded 'the brotherhood' was for the benefit of those wishing to follow the Moravian doctrine. It was not the intention that future bishops and ministers of the faith would give top priority to channeling resources from the church into avenues resulting in personal comfort, coerce older members of respective congregations to part with much needed resources so that resident pastors can improve personal wealth or control larger shares of available scarce resources. Happiness within the faith is about maximizing mutual benefits that supports feelings of well being for members of the church community, not just those at the top of the ministry!

Jesus taught, "For whosoever will save his life shall lose it: and whosoever shall lose his life for my sake shall find it. For what is a man profited, if he shall gain the whole world, and lose his own soul? Or what shall a man give in exchange for his soul [or life]?" (Matthew 16-25-26). Life is far more valuable than possessing even all the world, but if we live a purely selfish life we will lose it. In Matthew 10:39, Jesus taught: "He that findeth his life shall lose it: and he that loseth his life for my sake shall find it".

Zinzendorf equated life with the brotherhood and interpreted what Jesus meant, "Was that worldly things are short-lived, but life without those things, because of one's belief in Him, will make it more fulfilling, rewarding and happy." The way to that life, he showed: "Whosoever will come after me, let him deny himself, and take up his cross, and follow me. (Mark 8-34). Tell that to the Moravian priesthood of any rank! Jesus denied himself so as, to be totally obedient to God, His Father, even to death upon a cruel Roman cross. However, God raised him from the dead and gave him eternal life, divine glory with great honour, to sit at God's right hand in heaven, with "angels, principalities and powers being subject to him".

Clearly, Jesus wanted his disciples and by extension, those who profess to be his workers, i.e. men of the cloth, to know an extremely important truth about life and happiness. Denying self is to believe and obeying God is the way to life and happiness. Moravian ministers of the cloth will begin to walk that way when they respond to The Great Teacher's appeal in Matthew 11, 28-30: "Come unto me, all ye that labour and are heavy laden, and I will give you rest. Because by the time they get there, they will have completely forgotten what labour is and the only thing of heavy laden-ness will be their consciences, if that is still in vogue among the minister set! Indeed, they believe in taking their rest before they come unto him.

The humble, selfless, teachable person who allows him/herself to be disciplined by God's word is the really happy one - not the one who lives for 'number one' - for self! The first type is the God-centered, and worships God; the second type is self-oriented and only worships self! Typical of the modern Moravian set, whom it is difficult to believe when they imitate evangelical television bishops who run up and down stages shouting the name of the saviour "Jesus, Jesus" repeatedly! For that type of clown, or at best actor, the following quote from (Matthew, 7, 21) is appropriate, "Not everyone who says to me, 'Lord, Lord,' shall enter the kingdom of heaven, but he who does the will of my Father in heaven."

Denying self, coming unto Christ, learning of him, resting in Him, taking up His cross, copying His service to God and to others – these are the steps to a life of enduring happiness and peace. Jesus told his disciples, "These things I have spoken unto you, that in me ye might have peace. In the world ye shall have tribulation: but be of good cheer; I have overcome the world", John 16-33.

Jesus did not promise that His ministry would provide 'a bed of roses' in waiting for His Kingdom, he promised guidance, help, producing peace of mind and true happiness in his service. How can those professing, to be members of his ministry ever discover the fruits of that promise if they fail or do not attempt to lead the life, they were ordained to do. Can it be that they were never persons of requisite caliber or suited for such roles in the first place? Like modern day Moravian ministers who display good qualities to qualify as church Mafioso; they saw what there was, thought that they could please themselves, do what they liked with it and without concern for anyone or the sanctity of anything, plunged in and hastened the demise of what was there in the first place! They are truly religious thugs or hoodlums!

There will come to us an inner peace and happiness in the knowledge that God is our Heavenly Father, that he loves us, cares for us, forgives and helps us; that Jesus is our High Priest in heaven, who intercedes to God on our behalf, and that God's Kingdom is to come soon here on earth. At least that is what the pastor who occupies our church, remind us repeatedly and repetitively of, during his sermons! He however, 'talks the talk' but fails desperately to 'walk the walk'!

The original Moravians from Europe believed that the happy life is the selfless life, lived in the trust and to the glory of God. When we know The Father, "the one true God", we will come to love Him, "Who first loved us" and gave His son to redeem us from sins.

Words coming from our Lord's ministry explain godly happiness, access to it and how to obtain it. (Matthew 5, 1-16). The "poor in spirit, mourners, meek, those who hunger and thirst for righteousness, merciful, pure in heart, peacemakers, persecuted for righteousness' sake, reviled for Christ's sake", all have assured rewards. Jesus is not only encouraging his followers to seek true happiness, but is saying that their attitude and service to him guarantees happiness. The Moravian mafia cannot wait, giving every sign that they want theirs now! Here, while they can still enjoy it in the flesh!

The Greek word "blessed", when translated means "blissfully happy". The Lord Jesus promised that real, lasting happiness, along with God's provision of all our essential needs, will be ours, if we "seek first the Kingdom of God and His righteousness", Matthew 6, 33. That search is through reading God's word and earnestly praying to Him.

Happiness is the natural and spontaneous response to God's free and gracious gift of salvation. Shawe quotes Zinzendorf: 'There is a difference between a genuine Pietist and a genuine Moravian. The Pietist has his sin in the foreground and looks at the wounds of Jesus; the Moravian has the wounds in the forefront and looks from them upon his sin. The Pietist in his timidity is comforted by the wounds; the Moravian in his happiness is shamed by his sin'.

From the Moravian ideal perspective, happiness directly relates to the 'feel good' factor that worshippers experience as results of their 'in church' and common worship involvement. The serenity resulting from that is like a cloak, which forms an invisible aura around those blessed with that sensation. Thus, the happiness that one leaves the assembly of the Lord with translates into serenity, forming a mantle of cleansing and provides feelings of renewal. Those emotions begin on Sundays immediately after service and erode gradually as the week progresses when the inescapable sins of life resume their usual contamination that accompanies human existence.

Lay members of congregations may be forgiven for thinking that modern Moravian ministers deliberately seek to remove the happiness aspect from services and strive to make the lot of their congregation, at best confusing, in the long term. Yes, with their 'jump-up' music, they appease the young and innocent but that effect only lasts as long as the music. Afterwards, the target appeased switch off from what ever else is happening inside respective churches! It is not that a single member of the group is one rogue minister and has lost his/her way. There are lots of them, mainly Antiguans, forming a group disruptors sanctioned by the system, who do not care; transmitting vibes that those who do not like what they do and don't agree with their plan, can please themselves, in other words 'like it or lump it' would be a good motto for attitudes of that rebel group.

It is the elderly members of congregations, who suffer, mostly in silence and they do so, because they do not know what to do while the transformation from Moravianism to evangelical practice is in progress, if indeed, they recognize what is happening while the process is underway. Those older souls are desperately lost, having invested their life's service to Christ by means of the Moravian medium. Then, before they realize what is going on, find themselves in an evangelical organization, complete with big drums, guitar, piano, symbols going off all over the place with jumping ups in abundance and the occasional trumpet or saxophone to sweeten the melee! At which point the organist gets a breather. Sometimes, even during the sermon, the preacher has to revert to a fast beat, jump-up tune to get him/her into the desired frame of mind. It is a tremendous shock to the systems for senior persons finding themselves carried away by fake euphoria! What was a lifetime of worshipping God, trough dedicated meditation in serene settings is yanked away. Sermons that used to be enlightening, interesting thoughtfully delivered with genuine concern are gone; replaced by ministers screaming like banshees, waving fists, thumping things that shock individuals, making them hold onto seats for fear that the preacher would do something harmful to himself, the furniture or is about to have an epileptic fit of some order. Thus, what used to be 'attention to' and 'concentration on', aspects of sermons switches to focus on the antics of the preaching minister, performing idiotic dances with frantic tantrums. It used to be that persons remembered and discussed aspects of the sermon after church, individuals met inside churches or walked together afterwards, speaking to one another about points made in sermons, such observations would form bases of conversations for Moravians long after Sunday services ended. They would exhibit happiness through pleasant smiles on faces as they reminded each other of truisms touched on during sermons' deliveries. Now a days, after services, it is difficult to find leavers who can remember what the pastor was talking about, that is immediately after service and in spite of the fact that the modern Moravian minister tends to shout a lot! There is the tale about one of them who shouted, 'ranted and raved' for a long period and even though there were repetitions galore; afterwards, those asked about the message, failed to remember or understand what the minister said. That was not at all surprising, since the delivery and diction worked against comprehension.

Maybe it is just as well that not much attention to what the modern Moravian minister says in his/her sermon anymore, for too high a proportion of their utterances are biblically incorrect, fraught with self-induced pronouncements of what God wants the congregation to do, especially when there are possible spin-offs for the preacher.

Happiness with one's religious life should transcend the church and services into the realms of personal life, which is the original intended idea arrived at through the Moravian faith. It is a pity that our young and modern ministers, especially those from Antigua, do not pass on that idea of how to be happy the Moravian way to the youth of today. The misguided notion that feeding young people more of what they already get elsewhere, using different lyrics to make the 'jump-up' tunes sound catchy in church is mistaken. It is clear that approach just does not work. What some of the young ones now do is leave the service after the 'jump-up' segment ends, either for other venues or to socialize outside, in the church grounds. That is, after what they came for finish, they are gone, leaves the church for some other activity. Had more effort been invested, in teaching and explaining about real 'Moravian to goodness happiness', the church community would have been the healthier for it. That though, is the outcome of laziness on ministers' part! Once they lost interest in Sunday schools, the 'rut' moved in rapidly and Moravian happiness ebbed away, leaked out! Now the Moravian ethic is in danger of being lost for all time, at least in this part of the globe! Please God, where it still exists, if at all; save the former sense of happiness that existed in our church ?

The Ideal of Unintrusiveness:

This ideal is third in the Moravian ethos set, the belief that God positively wills the existence of a variety of churches to cater for different spiritual needs, indicating there is no need to win converts from other churches. The source of Christian unity is not legal form but everyone's heart-relationship with the Saviour.

That quality implies that there are, numerous ways of worshiping God and views about probable returns that can be expected, from service to the Father, who art in heaven! It places morale obligations on Moravian ministers and preachers to pitch their work so that it does not interfere with what ordinary Moravians want from their interaction with their maker and mediums to him. Moravianism is to do with the sanctity of one's personal attitude their own belief whilst inside the family of church members! It does not give them, the ordained minister set, license to trample all over people's beliefs. On the contrary, a person's system of approaches to God should be respected and nurtured once developed. In the process of development however, before and after confirmation, the minister's educational role is crucial. It involves the task of training young and developing persons about the power of the Moravian faith, its attitude to divinity and salvation. Emphasizing the need to live the life that Jesus Christ taught when he was here on this earth and how that message still has resonance to the quality of life, which can be enjoyed in this present age.

Guidance into this dimension of unintrusivity has to be from individuals who thoroughly understand the first two ideals. They must have good grasps of what is meant by simplicity, the need to keep matters of faith simple, including its translation into principles of learning and how it affects religious beliefs of others. That also has implications for interpreting biblical text, which can be very complex. Thus, simplicity spans well beyond the conduct of services but it also involves teaching, guidance and example.

Leaders of the faith with responsibility for developing young minds along paths to appreciating the third ideal of unintrusiveness must also be well familiar with the second ideal. What it is to be happy with the spiritual foundation, which is part of the Moravian approach to salvation. It is no good to take the present crop of ministers with 'self' as their focus of worship and rely on them to pass on issues of high morale importance to young, religiously innocent minds. From their performance, it is doubtful that they, the pastors themselves have any kind of appreciation for the notion represented by this ideal of unintrusiveness. It may be necessary to return to basics of Moravianism, once appreciation of the first two ideals have sunk in,; this third important principle can then be tackled.

At this point, it is appropriate to introduce the Moravian motto: "In essentials, unity; in nonessentials, liberty; and in all things, charity". Clearly, the 'unintrusive' ideal strongly underlines that motto. The first part, stating, 'In essentials unity', intends that there should be respect for the sanctity of personal religious belief, since that has to be one of the major essentials among the collection and as such deserves protection from those who would attack it. If there is to be unity in that part of the Moravian ethic; it has to mean that the church respects whatever individual members feel about their particular salvation or put another way, if there are differences in personal choices of serving God; no minister has the right to trample over that right to personal selection. Therefore, when one particular approach is too repeatedly and repetitively subject congregations with one theme, to the exclusion of other doctrines; that is a bias against the concept of unity in essentials. A fair approach would be for the resident pastor to discover what the range of beliefs amongst his flock is and then seek to service each position with equity!

The second part of the motto, "in nonessentials, liberty," strongly implies individual freedom to ideas and notions of their faith. It extends to interpretations about teachings of the Lord and Saviour Jesus Christ. Whatever one's theoretical ideas of what the Lord's teachings were, certain historical references need consideration in attempting to interpret what the real teachings of Jesus Christ could have been or meant. Yes, the bible exists, is widely considered as the true and only source of God's word. However, already it was shown that certain aspects of the good book were used to support unsavoury practices, suggesting there are occasions when extreme care, need to be exercised when using the bible as the sole reference. Another aspect of using the bible as the only source of reference that needs attention when approaching decisions about faith and beliefs is the consideration of possible routes included texts took to positions in it: its compilation and implications for plausibility when the initial sifting process is analyzed. Arriving at positions about one's system of beliefs is an area, which in closed societies can be very private. Even though there is acceptance of certain aspects about the life of Jesus, there can be suspicions that prescribed biblical messages surviving today as factual may not be the only, complete or accurate stories about what really happened millenniums ago! For example, the bible credits 'Paul of Tarsus' as the agent who worked extremely hard to spread the word of Jesus that we know today from his numerous letters. They explain how 'he saw the light' whilst on the road to Damascus, after he was redirected by the Saviour. However, who is to say that Paul did not suffer an epileptic fit and altered his real experience to suit his purpose that is now history?

In considering the collection origins of books, now universally known as 'the bible'. Logic demands that consideration of the fact that it was over three centuries after Christ lived, at around AD 325, when Constantine the Great organized the First Council of Nicea and gave it the task of separating divinely inspired writings from those of questionable origins. At that time, all such writings must have been in the same category!

In that act alone, there was ample scope for errors, especially since over 300 priests of varying beliefs were involved in that sifting process.

The potential for confusion, disagreement, deals, bartering and other acts of compromise were rife and ripe for abuse!

The actual compilation of the Bible was an incredibly complicated project involving churchmen of varying beliefs, in a background atmosphere of dissension, jealousy, intolerance, persecution and bigotry.

The topical and controversial issue of that time was the divinity of Jesus and that issue split the church into two main factions, each with many its own problematic sub-divisions. Constantine offered to make the little-known Christian sect the official state religion if the Christians would settle their differences. Apparently, he did not particularly care what they believed, as long as they agreed upon a belief, what ever it was. The idea of compiling a book of sacred writings was of paramount importance because Constantine thought that such a book would give authority to the new church he was in the process of sponsoring. There were many books by supposed prophets floating around up to about 312 CE, when the Council of Nicea decided which books were scripture and the remainder for the bon fire. Thanks to the notorious habit of early Christian leaders for destroying non-approved scrolls. We may never know what doctrines existed before the surviving document emerged; what real range of beliefs prevailed then, weather the result produced by the Council of Nicea was the best that could be obtained or indeed, how accurate it was.

Actually, legend has it that at the Council of Nicea, Constantine was unsure of what to include as Holy Scriptures from the batch, which later became the Bible. He threw the batch that he was to choose from onto a table. Those that remained on the table went in and those that fell off were not. There was also a report that at the time, Constantine the Great had three hundred different versions of the bible burnt. Think of al the information denied of or robbed from later generations, by sanctimonious, self-appointed editors from that bygone age and they were not even around, when Christ lived!

Indeed, in recent times, discoveries of ancient texts give glimpses into some ideas that date back to the time when work went into compiling the bible. Those newly found scripts indicate that the biblical version of Christ teachings slants in the bias suggested by the gospels of Matthew, Mark, Luke and John.

Recent findings, especially those from 'Nag Hamahdi', Egypt, suggest that the message from Christ was more logical, realistic, earthly and rational, compared to current evolved strands, molded into fodder for outrageous blackmail acts by unscrupulous ministers, who make a life practice of promising after life existences which cannot be substantiated or even tested so that perpetual deceptions are supported by attitudes spawned by religious blackmailers! How can it be possible to verify or check that the much sought after 'life in heaven', after this one ends, is a real option? Especially vulnerable are seniors in their twilight years, with desires to cling to present life so much that any remote promise of another go at living in some other exotic existence, cannot fail but be attractive to those of such mindsets. Thus, religious leaders in the caliber group of the Moravian Mafioso are having a great time, because of the propensity to believe religious ministers and the automatic trust they receive by virtue of their calling and so, when they make utterances pertaining to promises of after life; the tendency is to believe them! Supposed men and women of God are generally assumed to be blessed with 'inside knowledge' of what the Almighty thinks, wants and utters. Ministers are therefore uniquely positioned to take advantage of the type of evangelical doctrines, which seek to remove the unintrusive quality that should be part of the Moravian approach to worshiping God.

This third ideal of unintrusiveness, according to Bishop Shawe is a strange word to name a gift of God! Perhaps the best way to understand this gift is to say that Moravians historically have chosen not to impose themselves upon others in witness and service for Christ, but rather to seek opportunities to share our faith in ways, where at times it can best be received and appreciated. Perhaps, this ideal ought to be redefined as a gift of respect - respect for those with whom we differ, whether in matters of faith and belief or matters of policy and practice. Respect for the spiritual journeys of others has enabled long standing Moravians to play a significant role in worldwide ecumenical efforts over the years. It is worthy of note that there are those of the faith who refer to Zinzendorf as an ecumenical pioneer and even when ecumenical involvement placed Moravians in a minority position of dissent, they have stuck with it. Because, the prayer of Jesus, from the Gospel of John, which says, "I ask not only on behalf of these, but also on behalf of those who will believe in me through their word, that they may all be one." (John 17:20-21)

Perhaps a word of qualification is in order - we dare not think that unintrusiveness or respect for other beliefs means timidity or lack of zeal for sharing our thoughts on matters religious. Rather, it informs the *way* we share, and the spirit that underlies our testimony. I give thanks to God for the gift of uninstrusiveness - respect for those with whom we differ.

That philosophical conclusion leads into thoughts such as: If there is so much respect for other beliefs, why do mafia like, Moravian ministers flaunt so openly with evangelism and seek to immerse settled congregations with that idea? What is their aim? Since teachings from the heart of Moravianism paved the way for respect of each other's religious positions! Answers provided by modern wreckers of the faith, describe their movement as progress, they say that everything changes in time and that the Moravian church should be no different as far the evolutionary process goes, if other entities change; why not Moravians also? On the surface, it would seem that there is a modicum of truth in that premise. However, while change through natural dynamics is acceptable; change for 'copycat' reasons cannot be considered as serious development, more retrograde than anything else! Taking any Moravian church from a position based on Zinzendorf principles to one that mimics any of existing evangelic organizations cannot be evolutionary change; it is copying something already there, copying just for the sake of it. Somewhat like waking up one morning and announcing to the world that the wheel has just been discovered. Like the wheel, evangelical churches are 'ten to the penny'; the same is not true for Moravian churches. They are rare, once transformed into something else, cannot be recaptured or regenerated. The quality of Moravian ethos is not easy to replace, once bearers of 'the essentials' are no longer there. The copying effect is also reflected in the fact that everything evangelical centers do, the modern batch of Moravian hijackers follows suit: the evangelists get drums; Moravians buy drums also, the evangelists prolong jump-up sections of Sunday services; Moravian ministers also work those sessions into theirs as well, regardless of what the Moravian Book of Order' directs.

One facet that the 'sideway-church' is good at: they have the ability extracting tithes almost effortlessly from congregations. That feature drives the Moravian clergy berserk with jealousy! They knock themselves out in devising methods to encourage lay Moravians to adopt the tithing systems, so far to no avail. The introduction of that practice into the Moravian psyche was also attempted by the mafia set but not with much success though! One trait, Moravians at any level of fickleness has is and will not easily part with, is their stinginess. They will agree with whatever the minister says in face-to-face encounters but when it comes to parting with their cash; that is another matter! The Antigua mafia has yet to learn that about their local congregations. That is yet another example of how the unintrusive character of Moravianism has broken down and once more, testifies to the inherent greed of the clergical set.

It is blatantly obvious that changes taking place within a number of churches within the Moravian faith are not due to natural evolution but more akin to pushing the church into practices that appear to have increased earning potential. Once again, reasons for abusing another ideal can be pinned to greed of the clergy, who push these changes 'helter-skelter', hastening the demise of another long-standing ethic. Unintrusiveness, used to be a Moravian ideal but because of the now inherent greed; that quality had to go as part of their revolutionary experiments. The Moravian motto quite clearly says that as Moravians, the need to compete for souls with other churches should not be a part of the behaviour pattern but it now very firmly is. The church of late has grown to be very intrusive, resulting from the prevalent greed, rampant at all levels of the clergy.

The headlong rush to turn established Moravian churches into evangelical organizations or 'jump-up' centres has inevitably placed the organization into the market place for worshipers. Moravians are, now urged from pulpits to increase numbers of respective congregations by differing ruses. Ministers openly announce from pulpits, "bring someone else with you, bring the rest of your family with you" to such and such an event. When those sorts of instructions are issued, intended target groups are generally strangers, either from non-churchgoers or congregations of other denominations. In this dimension also, it is clear that on top of all else, modern Moravian ministers have added the quality of unconcern to the already long list of anti-Moravian standards. Indeed, that is a remark increasingly heard, from persons who understand what it is to be Moravians and know what they want from Sunday morning services. General comments of that kind, opines that not only the field ministers, but it is the majority of Moravian priesthood from the Caribbean region, including the bishops who, have entered a phase where everyone does exactly as he or she pleases, leaving abuses unchecked. Even edicts and directives from conferences of the church body go unaltered because their performance is peppered with intrinsic laziness, tardiness, bad pride and poor discipline. To this day, years old amendments do not see the light of any post office or box because somewhere there are officials failing at communicating important addendums. The consequential deterioration of performance resulting from that malaise is the gradual decay of those essentials mentioned in the Moravian motto. Therefore, continuous erosion of the necessary sustenance to keep the fibres of the faith resonating is bringing about the demise of the 'unintrusive' ideal, the Moravian ethos and indeed the church itself.

THE IDEAL OF FELLOWSHIP:

Moravian fellowship comes in many guises; there are numbers of entities that use the word fellowship as names or part of names. Indeed, in our church alone, three different applications of the word are in use and others that act out the concept as part of their functions. There is the 'Men's Fellowship' and the Women's Fellowship. Both erroneously used as money making devices rather than emphasizing the brotherly or sisterly qualities as the original intention was. Especially the Women's

Fellowship, whose officers meet church members outside church environs and instead of greeting them in church sisterly fashions by uttering a 'good morning' or 'afternoon', depending on the time of day; greets them instead with questions, such as: "What are you going to donate to the next church event?" Once a traumatized sister, having just left a doctor's office, was accosted in such a manner and the sister actually swore at the official. She was sorry afterwards but the temptation to swear was clear and the sister later asked God to forgive her.

By far the most popular mode of fellowship occurs during Sunday morning services, where congregations have short time slots at some point before reading biblical messages. It is a period, where worshipers physically greet each other, either through handshakes or as is becoming popular, bodily embraces, also called hugs. At fellowship sessions of that type, congregations are free to mingle inside and immediately outside the church walls while they interact together. Only the shy and anti-social types fail to enthusiastically involve themselves in those fellowship' greeting activities but in spite of that, most individuals, approached with extended arms, suggesting handshakes, hardly ever refuses, although that has been known to happen. However, the true Moravian, who understands and supports the Moravian motto, treats our local acts of fellowship as treasured parts of services. Indeed, some aspects of Moravian Sunday morning services are specially designed with ideas of enforcing fellowship activity: Palm Sundays are occasions when those special services attract dedicated and not so dedicated Moravians alike, as they look forward and join in the lusty singing of the 'Halleluiah Anthem', and "The Trumpet" on Easter Sundays following. In addition, other services that encourage fellowship-stirring renditions that make the blood of Moravians excite as individuals give them all they have vocally, spiritually and with enthusiastic involvement. Thus, as an ideal; the fellowship activity plays an importantly stirring role, when it is a part of the Sunday morning service and could be a great spiritual booster! Even on occasions when sermons fail to measure up to scratch, one could look back on the quality of the fellowship and be comforted by thoughts of, 'at least the fellowship was good!

At Moravian services, fellowship is free to all who wish to take part in them, at least for the present. That is not true for a number of faiths and churches. Some discriminate between who could take part in fellowship acts during any service and those not so allowed. Such establishments actually require that only members of their faith are eligible to join in their fellowship. They have a checking device, called a creed to ensure compliance. Creeds are yardsticks with which some churches and faiths encapsulate their beliefs, practices and standards. They ask 'who should be received by their Church to the enjoyment in their brand of fellowship?' Such organizations determine that consideration to be of significant practical importance and as such, it must attract controversy. Elders in such organizations opine that fellowship should be restricted only to members of their Church. It also has knock on effects, leading to other questions in which the original is embedded, namely 'Who has a right to membership in churches of that ilk?' In its response, the Church may require of the membership that they unite in profession of its faith and submit to her authority. The commitment to faith of their kind of church is what the church's creed or 'confession of faith' entails. Consequently, the ground of admission to membership in such churches is the adoption of her creed,—or, in other words, union with the Church in the profession of the faith and subjection to her authority. Unless individual members make that implied commitment, participation in fellowship acts will be denied them.

It follows therefore, in such strict act of fellowship, churches adhering to that practice are choosy about who they embrace in their fold and not only that but they are also selective with whom they fellowship. Imagine the embarrassment to anyone visiting a service of such a church. As a visitor, during fellowship time, none of the regular members would offer to greet or acknowledge the visitor. Such embarrassment would be even more pronounced if that visitor, were guest of a fully-fledged member. The effect would be that members with houseguests would not be able to invite them to Sunday services and the implications continue.

The above demonstrates that the use of a creed is a device that gives a certain amount of snob value to churches that have use of them. It serves on the one hand to make practitioners of that creed feel superior to others who do not share the faith, with the effect that it would encourage non-members to be ostracized by such discriminating practices. The extended logic being the hope that such practices would appear so exclusive to be attractive to strangers and encourage them into becoming members. To the mature person of dignity and integrity, such a device would be a definite turn-off; however, to the young, it could be like nectar to honey bees, especially if there are members of opposite sexes who are pursued by non-members. They can and are used as human bait to increase membership because the sought after members would be properly schooled in qualities of membership and entrapment. They can have suitors inside that church quicker than one can say, "Gotcha!"

If all who profess the name of Christ understood the Bible in the same sense and interpreted the Bible in the same way, a creed distinct from the Bible would be unnecessary. In such events, those circumstances would qualify as a creed, accordingly that general acceptance would be a summary of certain principles adopted by the parent association of individuals as articles of belief, by which they agree to abide. The word is of Latin origin, derived from the verb *credo* (I believe). According to ecclesiastical usage, a creed is an exhibition in human language of what its framers believe to be the great doctrines of the Bible. It is a formula of the faith; it possesses no authority in its own right, but derives existence and all the regard to which it lays claim from the Bible. The sense of any creed does not profess to make known anything, which was not already revealed neither does it undertake to constitute any truth, which was not truth before. Its purpose is simply to draw forth from the word of God great truths therein revealed, and state them in plain, intelligible language with certain bias that enhances beliefs of the faith that supports its framing.

Thus, a creed lends itself for use as a device of entrapment, it desires that members adopt common beliefs before they can claim acceptance to the parent church organization. It takes away the individuality of members, not only their biblical interpretation, also in 'form and depth' that individuals' beliefs should take, once instilled, it never to changes until and unless the collective changes. Such entrapment is similar to religious communism: 'All for one system of beliefs and one system of beliefs for all!' That is regardless of what one's private thoughts, motives or drives are. The creed representing the mother faith sees to those qualities for the individual. It relieves them of the necessity to think for one's self! If over time, it transpires that new ideas and thoughts visit any so indoctrinated and they dare to adopt such notions or put them into practice, such daring acts are tantamount to something approaching treason, certainly betrayal and deemed grounds for lifetime ostracism by the parent faith.

The Moravian faith, do not have creeds and for that we can all say, 'Thank God!' It has to be acknowledged that the Brotherhood's founding fathers knew what they were about when those men with foresight and courage, fought to break away from the Roman Catholics, whose religious practices were bogged down with traps in forms of creeds and were added to regularly. It was positively stifling!

For Moravians, it is sufficient that the motto places emphasis on importance of fundamental beliefs while expressing brotherly love and tolerance for differing views on such matters. The motto calls these 'The Essentials'. The Moravian Church has no formal creed; liturgies express the faith in the Lord Jesus Christ and promises of the Saviour. The Holy Bible remains the guide for Christian faith and living. It provides for and sanctifies freedom of belief among individuals. It protects for members of the faith, rights to choose what thoughts to invest beliefs and trust in.

In English, the word "fellowship" suggests sociability, camaraderie, perhaps a friendly romp with 'jump-up' music, cake and drink in the churchyard. Church fellowship then becomes a particular case, a kind of 'religious version' for the general category of friendly togetherness. Actually, that can be a misunderstanding. Church fellowship is not only a particular form of "fellowship". In general, it does not have to be about relations among people. It is the fellowship peculiar to the church. Another word for it would be "communion," not to be confused with holy-communion. Churches (and therefore their individual members) either are, perhaps are not in communion or in fellowship with each other. What does this mean? It depends on how one thinks about the church. Is it basically, a visible organization, or hierarchy with a God-given chain of command? Then church fellowship will depend largely on joint bureaucratic structures-for example, the so-called "historic episcopate" (the line of bishops stretching, without breaks supposedly, from the present all the way back to the founding fathers). Or, is the church a direct spirit-to-spirit affair, without real outward means of grace? In that case, her presence can only be guessed at, wherever people seem to be, especially when what they are doing appears to be "spiritual". Then the "visible church" is the outward company of the "obedient" and has no necessary connection to the "real" or "invisible" church. It is difficult to escape the view that the hijacking of Moravian churches is taking Moravianism in that direction, before our very eyes and almost unnoticed, except by few who lacks motivation to do anything about it!

The Moravian Church accepts neither of those extremes. 'The *Augsburg Confession*, Article Seven', has the distinction of being the first dogmatic definition of the church in the history of it. Until 1530, the Catholic Church was content to confess, with the Nicene Creed, that there is "one holy catholic and apostolic church". At Augsburg, the Lutherans had to make a new start, because all structural, bureaucratic attempts to secure unity of the church and truthfulness of her proclamations broke down. Article 7 goes to the 'heart of the matter' when it defines the church as 'the assembly of believers, in which the Gospel is purely taught and the sacraments are rightly administered.' Here, just as in the New Testament itself, the whole people of God are joined to His whole saving truth. Because there is only one Christ, there is only one church, which is His body. By faith alone, people are in Christ and are thereby members of His body. The branches are in communion with each other only because they are 'first of all,' in communion with the Vine Himself, the Source of all spiritual life (St. John 15:1-8). This one church and fellowship, or communion in Christ, has two aspects, an inner and an outer: "The church is not **only** an association of outward things and rites like other civic organizations, but it is principally an association of faith with the Holy Spirit in the hearts of persons. It nevertheless has its external marks so that it can be recognized, namely the pure teaching of the gospel and the administration of the sacraments in harmony with the gospel of Christ".

The means of grace (which are the preached and sacramental forms of the gospel) keep the two aspects of the Church from breaking apart into separate "visible" and "invisible" churches. The Church is an inner fellowship of faith with the Holy Spirit. However, faith and the Holy Spirit come only through the outward means: preaching, baptism and Holy Communion. The Church is an article of faith, we cannot see but must believe the one "holy Temple in the Lord" (Eph. 2:21). The foundation, that is teachings and sacraments of "apostles and prophets with Jesus Christ Himself as the Chief Cornerstone" (v. 20).

Two vital questions now need to be answered: (1) what is church fellowship? (2) What are its basis and limits?

The Greek "*koinoonia*" (fellowship, communion) means sharing, participating in common treasures, culminating in *the* communion of the Lord's body and blood (I Cor. 10:16). Only God can see the inner unity of all Christians in Christ. Church fellowship is about what we can see and know: joint administration and participation in the treasures of the gospel by which the church comes into being and by which alone, she is preserved. It means that church fellowship is essentially pulpit and altar fellowship, which then expresses itself in various concrete ways, such as joint services, missions and the like.

What is the proper basis for God-pleasing church fellowship? There can be only one answer that is necessary in the face of modern ecumenical confusion: "It is enough for true unity of the Christian church that the Gospel be unanimously preached there according to its pure understanding and the sacraments be administered in accordance with the divine Word. It is not necessary for the purpose of true unity of the Christian faith that everywhere uniform ceremonies, instituted by men, be observed …" (*Augsburg Confession*, VII, 2, 3,). This is the distinctively evangelical contribution of Moravian confusion. Nothing less than the pure doctrine and sacraments of the Gospel will do; also, nothing more than that is required for true unity and therefore for church fellowship.

Churches that teach or practice contrary to the revealed apostolic doctrine of Holy Scripture thereby stamp themselves as sectarian bodies, with which those who confess apostolic teaching are reluctant to practice fellowship. That happens all the time in our Moravian Sunday morning services; whenever a time snag happens; the first to be jettisoned is fellowship time.

This does not mean that no genuine Christians exists in sectarian bodies. On the contrary, there are fine Christians by the millions, for instance, in Roman Catholic, Eastern Orthodox, Baptist, and other Trinitarian churches (those that confess the Holy Trinity as the only true God). However, they faithfully oppose other official regimes as false doctrines (false, sectarian churches as such). Though refusing to make common cause with them in church fellowship, does not mean hating or despising the dear people of God, hidden and oppressed as they are under false teachers! Moravians understand themselves as guarding the apostolic truths of the Gospel on two fronts: salvation by grace through faith alone, against the works-righteousness of Roman Catholicism on the one hand, and the holy means of grace, especially the true body and blood of the Lord in His Sacrament, on the other.

An even deeper division has opened up among the churches in recent times, where inspiration and authority of Holy Scriptures as the Word of God is abandoned in exchange for excesses of evangelical churches. That is also the sad state of much of today's "local Moravianism", represented by the "Moravian mafia". When homosexual "clergies" impose gay functionaries on congregations in their power, it is difficult to envisage any deeper degradation of such "churches."

Church fellowship is in practice undergoing attacks to the church's immune system. Where the clear Word of God no longer determines the basis and limits of fellowship, but where opposition to that Word is, in principle, allowed or even welcomed. Such is equivalent to a spiritual counterpart of "AIDS". It robs the church in question of its ability to defend itself against any and all deadly infections (see Eph. 4:14). The Bible has much to say about "earnestly [contending, fighting] for the faith which was once delivered unto the saints" (Jude 3, see also Eph. 6:10-18). That is not popular in an age that sneers at the whole idea of absolute truth. Moravians however, should cling to the Lord's truth, not for the sake of pedantic "correctness", but because His teaching alone is life giving and liberates from sin, death, and the devil (St. John 6:63.68; 8:31.32).

Symptoms as defined in the above passage are now in the process of infecting the Moravian psyche. There are clear signs of this in the attitudes and practices of 'sexually iffy' ministers parading doubtful sexual practitioners as offspring's, spouses or even partners and the uncertainties that surrounds personalities of that ilk, imposed on congregations cannot but otherwise affect the quality of practical fellowships .

THE IDEAL OF SERVICE:

This 'Ideal of Service' reflects the standard pertaining to its quality, evolved from the historical courageous foursome, who really is for all time, original Moravian icons. Though spread over time, their combination or cumulative effect of the ideal, reached the point where scholars identified the 'Ideal of Service' to be an important quality that is necessary for the ethos that defines Moravians.

Beginning with the stance left behind by John Wycliffe (known as the Morning star of the reformation) because he was the first person showing enough courage to speak out against papal excesses. Hus was the first in historical line, which eventually led to the Moravian faith. His understanding of Wycliffe's 'point of view' made him unwilling to accept the flaws, perceived to be, in the system's hierarchy, teaching and practices of the only church at the time. He refused to be any part of the pretence, which the entire church-led community functioned and pretended that all was well. Hus was a man with a high morale sense of awareness and felt strongly that his understanding of Christ's teachings and other biblical interpretations were closer to the truth than the official version. Even when he was under the threat of losing his life, Hus held to the belief that his understanding of the scriptures was more accurate than current teachings. Continually, after every invitation for him to recant his written ideas that went against the official line; he would respond with the reply, 'show me where in the bible, it demonstrates that I am wrong!' History does not reveal if the authorities ever made an effort to demonstrate that Hus was wrong, or does it reveal what exactly the dissatisfaction with his attitude was. They insisted that what he wrote was heresy and on that charge, they took away his life.

Next in line to sew seeds that eventually resulted in the Moravian faith was the priest and philosopher, Martin Luther who essentially changed the course of western civilization by initiating the 'Protestant Reformation'. He too was convinced that inherited notions from Wycliffe and Hus were more relative to life than what the Roman Empire dictated was the only way. Luther wrote his ideas into various treaties, disagreeing with the clerical establishment and his refusal to recant anything written, or ideas contained in them, eventually led to his ex-communication from the Roman Catholic priesthood. In any event, as his theses suggest, he was mentally and philosophically already moving away from the religious rigidity of the then, only established church. His determination to turn thoughts into action evolved into the development of the religious strand known as the Lutherans and to this day, that practice continues. Moravians developed along similar lines to the point where there are joint worship arrangements in geographical areas where both communities exist.

Moravians and Lutherans regard themselves as distinct members of a single flock who follow their Shepherd in mission and ministry. Their joint theme, portrayed by the emblem of "the Good Shepherd," following Jesus, with fellowship at the forefront of their common dialogue. Also present is the realization that this dialogue is unique for both churches. However, although the Lutherans have roots directly back to Martin Luther; Moravian philosophy and practice had to wait for Count Zinzendorf to get it moving at his village of Herrnhut, in Germany among a group of refugees from Moravia.

Zinzendorf was a man with a naturally alert, active mind, enthusiastic temperament that made his life one of ceaseless planning and executing plans. Like Martin Luther, he also, was often carried away by strong-vehement feelings and easily got upset by sorrow or joy. His talent for talking was well suited to continual search for truth, especially on religious subjects and even with those who held different views. Few men show more concern for the happiness and comforts of others, even with insignificant matters. His activities occasionally landed him in odd situations and led to contradictions that frequently looked like misleading or telling tall tales. The courtly training of his youth made him sensitive about his authority even when no one disputed it.

Experience brought out the oratorical qualities in him and though his dress was generally simple; his personal appearance encouraged airs of distinction and force. Such qualities caused misunderstandings about some of his projects and resulted in banishment from his first settlement in the province of Saxony. Twelve years after he was first banished from Herrnhut, the successful outcome from his initial efforts encouraged the government of the day to revise their earlier ban. Indeed, they went further and invited Count Zinzendorf to extend the experiment of what was the initial brotherhood community to other areas where he formed more settlements like that at Herrnhut and so the initial Moravian movement blossomed within a small geographical area in Germany. It was that initial success, which encouraged the Count to export his idea and message to other lands, thereby causing the seed of Moravianism to grow outside of mainland Europe.

It is an amazing deduction that the driving influence behind a germ of an idea visited only three persons in a time span of four hundred years, survived throughout those early centuries, amidst cultures that lacked reliable means of communication, even the art of writing was limited and available only among to a privileged few. From Wycliffe of the mid fourteenth century to Zinzendorf some four hundred years later, that germ of an idea spawned over that distance in time, visiting three men with almost identical courage, passions and skills that enabled them to interpret the works and teachings of Jesus Christ in exactly the same way.

They knew that Christ' ideas for life were indeed, the best way to live. Recognizing there was more to existence than living in hopes that were impossible to test and that humans understood best what they could feel, see and experience. Those visionary men realized that dogmatic insistence of looking to the sky as the place where humans could one day ascend after this life was hopefully flawed and misleading. Especially when existing science read other messages from the movement of heavenly bodies and useful intelligence gleaned from stars' combinations, conflicted with rules about uses of those same heavenly bodies by the church.

Creative ideas and common sense were at odds with suggested notions on that subject, especially since available science proved increasingly beneficial to life. Inevitably, studies and findings drove intelligent men of learning to question certain dogmatic positions held as indisputable facts. Thus, questions relative to situations of dogma, which defied logic and intellect, were bound to evolve! Progress of men's understanding meant it was no longer acceptable that matters of serious concern were brushed aside by bullying tactics or statements that suggested 'it was against God's wish that ordinary mortals should question his works.' When it became clear that answers of that type were indeed, attempts to avoid facing questions about matters embedded in mystique and ignorance. Defenders of the then 'status quo' tended to resort to hostile stances as the gist of questions heated their consciousnesses and ignorance. More so, when those defenders, themselves saw their logical defenses crumble before their very vivid imaginations. Then when assumed truths began to look shaky, they turned to intimidation, threats and bullying tactics, using devices such as ex-communication and even more gruesomely taking away lives form those who asked the most searching questions, branded them as heretics before removing their lives. Of course, once certain questions were out there, in the arena of life, killing off the odd inquisitive priest, monk or philosopher, did not mean that the question itself would go away. Quests for truths have odd habits of popping up at inconvenient times and places. While life prevails and there are individuals who do not understand aspects of it, they are going to ask questions, if answers do not satisfy causes for such questions, those same individuals will look for their own answers. Wycliffe, Hus and Luther were men of that caliber. They asked questions about interpretations that made little sense. Eventually, they had to look for answers from within their own resources, when satisfactory responses failed to be forthcoming; their impeccable logic led them to more sensible, meaningful and acceptable answers.

For example, one hot question spanning that period concerning the conflict of credibility about the teachings of Christ as documented in the existing New Testament canon. The only available witnesses of Christ's teachings, utterances and other performance, was officially documented in the four gospels, credited to Matthew, Mark, Luke and John. However, similarities of those books provided the basis of much cause for debate, especially in light of reports that compilation of the cannon happened over three hundred years after Christ lived. The compilation of it commenced on the initiative of Emperor Constantine with questionable assistance from the Council of Nicea. The initial task specified by Constantine was to produce a list of books that would give respectability and form the basis of the Christian Empire he was in the process of developing. That council had as members, three hundred clerics of varying religious paraphernalia and each with his own agenda. The intention was that they were supposed to work together to produce a religious document that would be used as the official Christian document and support Constantine's historical ambition to convert Rome from a pagan based society into one positioned on Christianity. The Council of Nicea had the daunting task of wading through the vast array of writings about what Jesus said, meant and did when he walked on this earth over three hundred years hence. The diversity and availability of Jesus relative texts were as widespread then as popular records are today, almost every day new releases about the Jesus' teachings were available in the Roman Capital and areas of high density, Christian populations. Thinking persons during those darkened ages, spanning the period from Wycliffe to Zinzendorf, believed that after so many generations, in terms of centuries, following the time when Christ's initial thoughts and intentions were actually delivered by Him; much room for error existed; either through mistaken serial interpretations or deliberate manipulations along the line. Three-to-four hundred years is a long time for mistakes to creep into anybody's story that was around for so long! Fact was that in the centuries between Christ's life and the compilation of the bible, many different versions of his life story, messages, utterances and deeds circulated, as indeed there were numerous interpretations of his miracles and teachings.

Dilemmas, passed down from Wycliffe, through four centuries via Hus, Luther and Zinzendorf reflected on, 'How were they supposed to know that humanity, after all that time, were not fooled by the winning canon of new testament books which emerged as the eventual final selection. A product that societies for nearly two thousand years, looked upon as a flawless, holy effort, presented to Christians as unique and of unquestionable truths. It also emerged that during the period of Nicean Council's activities, its three hundred members deliberated on which books to select and that deliberation began at around AD 325. However, it was not until AD 382 that Pope Damascus produced the first list of books for use as a working bible. Indeed, over one Millennium after Pope Damascus, Martin Luther wrote his own version of the bible, selecting from the surviving list of books. By that time, the destructive influences of the Constantine and Nicean Council combination saw to it that there were not any choices in New Testament gospels offering real alternatives to the only four in existence, about the teachings of Jesus.

Luther was also aware that Emperor Constantine was a man who killed people if they failed to do his bidding and this was what happened when the Emperor declared that certain scripts were not suitable material for inclusion in his book of religious collections, which would justify his Rome as a Christian state. Having issued decrees against inclusion of his list of banned books, the Emperor was not satisfied to leave things there, taking a leap forward, he threatened death to anyone caught with banned books. That stroke of his edict transformed non-acceptable scripts into illicit writings and many Christians domiciled in Rome or any part of Italy, lost their lives because they were discovered in possession of parchments classified as illegal. While Constantine's ban on scripts served to clean up circulating literature. It also forced many flourishing writers to seek other employment because that industry effectively dried up when the powers of the day had the authority to look at any piece of writing and without reference to anything else or anyone, had the power to declare the subject text legal or illegal. Those who wielded that kind of unquestionable authority possessed the means to pass death sentences on the spot. Within an atmosphere so highly charged with potential for intimidation, only the senseless, foolhardy or dim-witted would continue to write and publicize their writings. Holders of doubtful text sought release by burning; burying whatever scripts, they possessed to avoid becoming part of the next bonfire.

Luther and philosophers like him, through the ages, were conscious of choices available to express their interpretations of Christ's teachings but suffered similar disadvantages of not knowing what was missing from available range of scriptures, although they suspected that the working cannon could not have been complete. It was evident that the Apostle Paul had an almost monopolistic position on published letters in the canon, which was increasingly being accepted, by the Catholic establishment as the only and unquestionable version of God's word and emphasized those attributable to the Holy Trinity.

In his biblical version, Luther had no choice but to use text already available. Had he been alive today, he would have learnt that some of those hitherto banned documents were slowly returning to circulation, discovered by shepherd boys, villagers in search of cooking fuel and people who dig for artifacts. Previously unheard of gospels and other works, carbon dated to about the same period as canonized gospels reputedly were. Translations of discovered parchments indicate that Jesus teachings varied in substance, more widely than the New Testament canon reported for the past two millennia. It would appear that Jesus said much more and performed with extended flexibility according to the newly discovered documents. Not only have those newly discovered texts report differences to what previously pertained, they also indicate new meanings and emphasis. For example, the gospel according to Judas, reports that instead of behaving like a traitor as the New Testament suggests or how Roman Catholics like to portray him, he Judas, was actually carrying out the wishes of his Lord and master! Otherwise, what device would they have used to entrap Jesus before crucifying him? Thus, from the point of view of that gospel, Judas performed a useful function by arranging to identify Christ, in order for Jesus to have his blood shed for us sinners!

Thus, the ideal of service began with efforts of those four sequential pioneers who weaved one long successive path, through a mire of confusing scripts, deliberately spun to swing historical and biblical meanings so that future security of religious practices could perpetually work to indefinitely, control life for future generations!

Thank God for men of caliber as demonstrated by Wycliffe, Hus, Luther and Zinzendorf. That they had courage enough to ask honest questions, though not generally welcomed, tenaciously investigated and found solutions, which led to initiating concepts that today are identified as original and necessary for: 'The Ideal of Service'.

Unfortunately, in the present era, that ideal, along side many others, is in great danger of slipping through the framework of what passes for Moravianism, although that is already the case for some communities. Like the other major ideals, the sort of dedication and selfless commitment necessary for their survival, is swamped by institutionalized greed and other facets of avarice, which grew to be the dominant characteristic of those who function, inside this conference's Moravians priest set. Without evidence of the service ideal, the result is that the Moravian Mafia has abducted and killed Moravianism for dedicated Moravians. The pity is that the losers, who are age-old congregations, do not recognize the extent of damage those religious criminals have done to the faith. Unfortunately, those who do, lack resources to react against the Antiguan Moravian Mafia and their destructive ways!

The demise of the last ideal effectively ushers in the death knell of ethos, which define Moravianism. The dilemma that now prevails: within the range of practices and experiments perpetrated by ordained Moravian ministers inside of buildings, historically labeled as Moravian churches, with whatever sub titles precedes the Moravian definition. Even though practices acted out inside such establishments, are nowhere close to prescribed service order, listed in nominal 'Moravian Books of Order'. Yes, structures have not changed; however, since what goes on inside them do not resemble anything Moravian! Can routines that have changed so much together with original buildings continue under the classification Moravian? This writer thinks not! The structure is the home or place of worship, where persons attend services. Being Moravian involves taking part in a particular kind of ritual, shaped by the ethos, built upon the five ideals and if those ideals are obliterated, killed or mutilated beyond recognition, then the entity, founded on those ideals must logically have been annihilated! Thus since the Moravian mafia have so brutally demolished those ideals, then they are guilty of murdering our Moravian faith and replaced it with practices which can be found in any 'ten-a-penny, side-way-church!' Therefore, in the spirit of Wycliffe, Hus, Luther and Zinzendorf, what those imposters, who are supposed to be ordained women or men of the cloth, have done to the faith is sacrilege! They are therefore, properly labeled: "The Moravian Mafia"!

CHAPTER THREE,
MORAVIAN GOVERNMENT.

I became a Moravian shortly after birth in that the woman who brought me into this world christened me in the local Moravian church. Her mother was Antiguan; seems that many of our local Moravian community have Antiguan ancestors. As a toddler the mater, being a single parent deposited me each weekday at the local Moravian crèche, more recently known as the Moravian pre-school. For the early years of life, had to attend Sunday services at eleven of the clock each Sunday, thereafter, return home for the midday meal, then back to the same building, in time for Sunday school at two in the afternoon. At the time of writing, there are only a handful of us veterans from those days left and even fewer grown-up members from that time. The latter group is now octogenarians and can no longer attend services, because in their words, "The minister goes on for too long!" they, like some of us younger-sters have to take medication at precise times. The current pastor does not show concern for our predicament, even though he knew about it, although the previous pastor, greedy as he was, did.

My confirmation along with a number from the present congregation occurred when we were twelve years old. For that event, my mother skimped and saved in order to buy my first boyhood suit of white, albeit cheap flour-bag material and with short pants. Can't say that it was any kind of joyous occasion, being too young to have that kind of sensitivity but I was proud of my new flour-bag, white suit. What I remember though was the thought of protesting against directions from the maternal home never occurred to me. Indeed, there was comfort in the company of my potential fellow communicants and a certain amount of pride to being labeled a Moravian. Even though I did not know what it meant then. None of us did but I am sure that the good bishop told us, during one of those pre-confirmation classes we had to attend each week.

In those days, Sunday church services ran for exactly one hour, from eleven to twelve o'clock and were structured as the 'Book of Order' prescribes: 'opening hymn, Litany or Liturgy, a lesson, either a canticle or hymn, another lesson, another hymn, the sermon, followed by the last hymn and finally the benediction. Without fail, the then bishop finished his services bang on midday, never failed, even when there were visiting preachers or christenings; dispensations of Holy Communion took minutes longer than normal services. Finishing time was generally the same for Sunday services; thereby, conforming to the simplicity ideal of the Moravian ethos. That memory contrasts with what pertains today: there s no definite time duration for services anymore. Most Sundays, congregations are lucky if they escape from the church building in less than three hours after services commence. Once I witnessed the minister arrive one whole hour after service began, then proceeded to hold the congregation captive for over two hours after performing his television glitz style entrance into the service.

Looking back, I recall that my youthful church days were times when priests serving Moravian churches had training for their roles. Now-a-days, individuals recruited from theoretical training and then set loose on Moravian congregations, without schooling in the habits or expectations of Moravians. Small wonder they get confused when confronted with genuine Moravians. I am convinced that they honest-to-God, do not know what to do or how to behave with Moravians. It appears that for them, those unenlightened pastors, it is a matter of learning as they go along, like putting a learner-driver in a vehicle with 'L – plates' on, handing over the key and leaving him to get on with it. Such an arrangement takes for granted the tolerance level of the poor, subject congregation. In that kind of situation, members effectively, are at the mercy of whoever the new but raw minister is. When such a minister thinks that he always know best, he will not be inclined to listen to advice from any of the subject congregation, not even the elected chairman and that is when life for the congregation get ugly and uncomfortable. Furthermore, if that minister displaying such arrogance happens to be the nominated superintendent, it makes the ongoing situation even more unbearable. In such a situation, the pastor sees himself as susceptible to God's control only. No one else receives any regard from him. In his head, he has become the local deity!

Such behaviour by one, who relies on any congregation for existential support including indirect remuneration, can only by tolerated by a church community with careless or sleepy congregations. Among such a group, attendance is partly for cosmetic reasons, giving impressions that they do not even know why they attend. I once carried out an experiment: immediately after church, asked a number of persons "what the sermon was about?" None of them knew. In terms of spiritual needs, church going is an activity, especially among so-called Moravians, where clients do not know their real purpose or care what it is. For some, it is something they were accustomed to doing at some previous existence and now that they are old or older; dances are no longer in vogue; they have nice clothes; so where better to wear them than to church? Quite a number believe that gong to church, places them in good standing with the Lord and enhances their chances of spending the 'after life' with him in his glorious kingdom. The latter is the very vulnerable set, when pitched in the light of unscrupulous ministers' greed. Pastors target them like homing pigeons. Pitching ever-mounting lists of demands under banners of support for God's work and the consciences of this group, allow themselves to be subjects of exploitation by ministers with more than their fair share of greed, arrogance and conceit. Seems that the older the member is, the more susceptible they become. I have known aged persons economize on food expenditure, so that they could meet demands from the church minister. To make matters worse, outrageous behaviour on the part of such ministers present them as strategies, disguised as fund raising. The fact that members, albeit elderly ones, at times do not have enough to eat is to such pastors, of no consequence, just so long as their pockets are full to the point of bursting is the limit of their concern. Consciousness of the atmosphere described, invokes ideas of what it must be like for persons living in societies where such performances are all pervasive. It is difficult to realize a church society where such dynamics prevail; it is easier to visualize that type of environment as one where dictators rule!

Feels like the new set of Moravian ministers have characters that approach similarity with those of dictators. The amazing thing is that the church community permits them to get away with that type of outrageous behaviour. Perhaps the term 'get away with' assumes senses of care by the congregation. Truth is, in most cases, church attendees are once-per-week creatures. That set attend Sunday morning services and only those, not regularly either. They therefore do not take seriously the needs of the church nor do they seriously consider the servicing requirements outlined as church's needs. The various demands or taxes imposed during services are forgotten, once outside. As soon as they leave the church building, whatever the latest begging program was, gets to be instantly jettisoned out of their minds. From a church point of view, it means that only the concerned members carry the financial burdens and that is why the frequency of demands are so keenly noticed. A point in case: there was this pastor of fairly recent stewardship, fancied himself as a hotshot, interior designer, got the idea to renovate the church décor, he convinced the fickle chairman about how nice the church would look and the potential of that new look for attracting new members. Neither the minister, Chairman or anyone else from the various committees sought to tell the minister that the cost of his ambitious plan was too much for the size of the congregation to bear. Even if they did, it is doubtful that he would listen, a common trait of the mafia minister set, once they have an idea, they do not listen to anything contrary or reasons why that idea may not be feasible. Some of us even suggested that a degree of recycling the old furniture be considered as part of his renovation plan. He would entertain no suggestion, other than what was in his mind. Anyway, this minister, over a longish period, in terms of months, went ahead, brought from another country, one who specialized in church interior décor and eventually produced a wonderfully presentable church inside. For months after, everyone who visited the sanctuary spoke about how nice it looked and for days after would form kernels for their conversations. Parties brought special events to the church for it truly was lovely to behold when the paint was yet wet and the vinyl upholstery was still shiny-new.

It was not until about eight months later, after the decorating minister left for pastures new, that the lay-church discovered the shock effect of the pastor's decorating experience, The result was felt in the extent of the church's overdraft with the bank was so great that it was impossible to do normal business using the standing current account. The replacement pastor together with the accounts person had to invent techniques of financial subterfuge, in order to conduct the church's business. The reason was that the décor minister managed to get the church into so much debt with his ambitious renovation plan. He did not bother forming any kind of special committee to monitor aspects of the project; single handedly, he pushed the project along. Even if the financial supervisor recognized what was going on, the strange loyalty to the pastor resulted in silence about what went on. In any event, church financial advisors are not in habits of speaking out of turn, with regards to church financial problems and the result was, for a long time, the congregation knew nothing about the financial plight of the church. To raise funds for the resultant overdraft, the minister drew up a means related plan to spread the debt among the members. Only God, himself and maybe the Chairman knew what the criteria was for demanding how much from whom. Registered members got substantial bills for varying amounts, depending on perceived social standing and profession or place of employment. What the décor minister discovered, whether he recognized it or not; was the nature of this particular Moravian sleepy character: during his planning of the renovation, to create excitement about the idea, the fore-note was initiated as church notice as initiation of the fund raising process. That initial drive was relentless, numbers of collections per service increased and wherever possible, funds from other causes were shunted into the pet project. In spite of that, the cash inflow, for the project receipts were much too slow for the pastor's taste. When his frustration with the rate of reserves build-up rose to a certain pitch; he went ahead with initiating the project, even before knowing whether there would be enough funds to pay for it. That was when the tax idea raised its head and written demands circulated during Sunday morning services as personalized letters.

That was where the sleepy 'church mentality' let the plan down. Only a few of us bothered with meeting the tax demands and that was not enough to cover the renovation cost. Most members who initially supported the idea vocally or with attitudes of approving looks and nods of encouragement, stopped well short of putting hands in pockets or writing checks for sums demanded. It was clear that the membership talked the talk but when it got to walking the walk, they ran the other way. The situation reached to the point where the church is now heavily in debt with an overdraft without a visible bottom, on account that it is so far out of sight.

That same church attitude of 'say one thing and mean another' is also evident in matters other than financial. Members vehemently complain to each other about the previous minister's extravagance but never to the minister himself. Since the arrival of this new mafia religious thug, most talk objectionably about his showbiz preaching style, how long and repetitive his sermons are; his rudeness and arrogance; as usual they don't do anything about their feelings. They would rather allow the transformation he is implementing to wash over them, suffer whatever manifestations their senses of protest registers than to take communal action to stop the rut. That collective attitude really is the fuel, which perpetuates the minister's outrageous behaviour. It keeps him going because reactions are judged as acceptable when in reality they are not. I sometimes wonder if the reaction just described is used by Moravian ministers, like politicians, in calculating or taken into consideration before willful pastors take it upon themselves to push their blatant attitudes onto unsuspecting congregations. Do they say to themselves, "Oh these people are not going do anything? I could do as I like!" Assuming the docility of those who go to church in good faith, albeit, not really knowing why they do. The dynamics are difficult to analyze. Knowing the state of my own attitude, the tendency for me would be: 'do as much that would be considered fair, for after all, it is indeed the responsibility of members to look after the church, including the welfare of its minister. Although, it might be an idea for the pampered Moravian clergy set to find other jobs instead of relying on the church to support them. After all pastors of sideway-churches earn independent livelihoods and since this Moravian set like to copy what sideway-churches do; they can jolly-well copy their work ethics also! Alas, they are such a lazy bunch; I will not hold my breath for them to look for paid employment. In spite of that, there should be a strong sense of equity in the allocation of financial duty towards the church. Not only amongst members, also ministers themselves, ought to have consciences about how much to expect from the church community. A big 'turn off' for me is when the minister radiates so much greed that he or she signals that their only concern is about what they want. Three times in as many years, I heard the same pastor announce to congregations, "I have an overdraft of Ten Thousand dollars. I want somebody to clear it for the church?" That kind of demand from the pulpit never fails to raise my blood pressure.

It is difficult to understand how ministers can behave in ways, suggesting that they can perform according to their own tastes and without regard to the needs of congregations. Guidelines about how Sunday morning services should be conducted is clearly prescribed at P400, in the 'Book of Order; yet still that routine had not been performed, not since the arrival of this new minister, nearly one year in duration at the time of writing. There have been several protests about that blatant neglect. However, dumb silence has always been the response. The minister blatantly advocates, "I am not going to argue with anybody!" He says, as he continues doing as he pleases. Another of his now famous utterances is, "Nobody is going to tell me what to preach or how long to preach!"

I have complained to the Chairman of the church so many times that whenever he, the Chairman sees me approaching along one route; he selects another in order to avoid meeting face-to-face. Indeed, because of my nuisance factor in complaining about the quality of Sunday morning services, the Chairman and his wife have made me a person to avoid.

Then the time came when enough had to be called enough. That was when I took disciplinary action against the church pastor, who is also Superintendent of the island conference.

The letter of application is reproduced below. As expected, six weeks after the application, no response has yet reached me, not even an acknowledgement of receipt, nothing from the bishop's seat. That has to be another clear indication that there is minimal control, if any, over Moravian pastors, in the field.

"Samuel Nathan,
Address supplied in the original.

Date supplied here.

The Chairman of the PEC,
The Moravian Church,
EWI Province,
Antigua,
West Indies.

DISCIPLINE.

I, Samuel Nathan, member of the Zion Moravian Church (Zion), Basseterre, St. Kitts, hereby file a report to the Provincial Elder's Conference (PEC) of these Moravian churches, against the pastor of

Zion and Island Conference Superintendent. My application is to have disciplinary action taken against the resident minister. In that, his performance and conduct are contrary to **P229, under 'Appeals',** citing items listed below.

Specifically, as pastor of Zion Moravian Church:-

a. The pastor has persistently disobeyed the 'Book of Order' for Moravian churches: At none of my attendances to Sunday morning services, has he ever conducted one service, as prescribed by the *'recognized order for Sunday services throughout the province'*, **P 400** *(Order of Worship and Liturgical Principles)*. Consequences of failure to observe that prescribed traditional form of service include enforced absences from Sunday morning church attendances by elderly members and those conditioned by specific medical needs with time relative medications; increased anxiety and distress to susceptible members.

b. He presides over the demise of traditional Moravian practices by his persistent failure to use the prescribed routine at Sunday morning services. The eventual outcome will be that Moravianism becomes unrecognizable in time and be lost to future generations when the character of Zion as a Moravian church would have been irretrievably lost and replaced with that of another evangelical church. If the accused reverend has an evangelistic zeal, he should find a church of that ilk to 'pastor to' and leave our Moravian church to continue with its traditional ethos. If he is allowed to continue with his experiment and change the character of Zion; future generations won't know what it is to be Moravians! Those of us who still value the traditional church will lose a valuable form of worship practice! Where will we go when Zion's Moravian style service, is taken away from us? The reverend should be honest and find himself an appropriate church for his calling, instead of experimenting with our established church, while enjoying the comforts of its privileges!

c. He is frequently late for Sunday morning services, once in excess of one hour; deliberately using entrance to worship, in the style of an actor making stage entrances for showy effects rather than portraying one who is charged with delivering spiritual uplift. Further, his continued use of the 'late tool', set bad examples to those young people he professes to be in tune with and often claim to favour.

d. His sermons are excessively long because of repetitive contents, often irrelevant to declared themes and quotes inaccurately from the bible, insulting intelligences of those who know our way around the good book. His presentation style is boring and unnecessarily loud, especially when attempts are made to mimic the television character of T. D. Jakes.

e. I deduced that he is not above bending the truth out of shape in order to obtain desired outcomes.

f. He dresses shabbily when off duty and silently fails to communicate his status as an ordained minister of the church.

g. His perpetual blunderings while conducting Sunday morning services occur regularly and are attributable to his casual approach to duties. The latest among which were the desecration of one Palm Sunday's singing of the 'Hallelujah Anthem' and then following that on Easter Sunday, his failure to properly coordinate the necessary trumpet players for singing of 'The Trumpet'. For the first time in living memory, the church sang 'The Trumpet' without support of trumpets. Yet trumpeters were available, arriving close to the end of service. The list of his blunders continues to mount, giving the impression of being a lazy, bungling incompetent who does not care about factors affecting his performance.

h. He displays defects in the compassion that comes from maturity, which is necessary in pasturing to an emotionally and spiritually diverse congregation.

i. His blinkered focus on youths to the discomfort of and unconcern for other groups within the congregation suggests a level of intolerance and 'lack of flexibility' that a man of the cloth must possess.

As superintendent of the Island Conference:-

a. To my knowledge in at least one instance, he failed to use expeditiously reasonable and sensible methods to resolve a problem that affected the wider community of island Moravians.

b. He fails and continues to neglect his responsibility of perpetuating Moravian practices within the island conference community, thereby eradicating centuries old style of ministry and sacraments. Removing from present congregations, opportunities to serve God the Moravian way and denying future generations the possibility of learning about what the Moravian approach to serving God is!

I submit that the items above are reasons why the incumbent pastor of Zion Moravian church and Superintendent of the island conference fails at administering correctly Moravian Church practices and procedures according to Moravian doctrine of the Word and Sacrament, defined at **P 400,** within the 'Book of Order' for Moravian churches!

I wish to proceed with disciplinary action against the defined minister for the above reasons, with the sincere desire to retrieve those treasured traditions, before it is too late!

In the name of our Lord and Saviour, Jesus Christ! Amen!

Respectfully,
Samuel Nathan.'

As suggested, the application for disciplinary action against a minister, considered to be extremely ignorant in terms of manners and various dimensions of knowledge bases, bible, Moravian ideals, its history, ethos and congregational concern. It is doubtful that it will see the 'light of day'. With reference to the fact that it is possible to ascertain that rain fell without actually seeing the rainfall; I have the same circumstantial confidence that nothing will come of the disciplinary request. The deduction therefore is that the mafia style ministers, sent to churches with top priorities of ensuring that 'cash flows' to their bishops' seats be maintained at all cost. Their instructions, it appears, contain highest emphasis on getting returns from field churches, over and above everything else, continuously back to the PEC coffers at its Antigua base. Returns are levees, locally called 'quotas'. The system of quota fixing equates to a form of taxation, allocated against each church in the province. Each separately assessed by PEC. The formula for calculating quotas is mysterious and in spite of requests from Moravian sources to obtain clarification about the general criteria of calculating it, no answer has been forthcoming. Note: there exists a superintendent for each island conference. However, the bishops at PEC give this particular aspect of church administration their personal touch, for that is the mechanism by which they get direct control of the money. Anyway, back to the story. Each church in the province receives its quota demand in time for the start of every calendar year, although each demand is for the entire year; expectation being that individual churches work out how the annual figure breaks down into monthly installments and has responsibility to ensure that payments get to PEC promptly. Note: sums of money used in this narrative are estimates, since no confirmation or input sought on this subject were returned. Three years ago the annual estimate for Zion was Eighty-Four Thousand dollars (XCD), equivalent to US$31,700.00. Worthy of note also is the fact that I have never seen any statement about how monies received by PEC are used and that is in spite of requests to various levels of church hierarchy, not even to acknowledge any of my requests. That indicates to me, there is some degree of secrecy surrounding expenditure habits, concerning monies demanded by Moravian church administrators. It could be that regional superintendents, even priests probably get to know about PEC's spending habits. If they do, it is one of the best-kept secrets from the grass roots of this church system! It has to be mentioned here that such a 'blip' in administration would not be surprising since the attitude that pervades the entire structure is one where no official appears to give a hoot for anything or procedure that does not affect them, even though there are 'feedback' aspects to actions taken; they do not even care about that! Bottom line is congregations perpetually have their noses rubbed in the need for PEC to get its quotas punctually and in full; however, there is no information as to how such quotas are spent, filtering through to the suppliers of it.

There are four main Moravian churches on the island plus another miniscule church, which shares a minister with one, larger and since Zion is the largest in the group, the expectation is that Zion's quota would be greater than the others on the island.

A reasonable average quota would be US$30,000.00 per church, each year and that figure increases annually. When returns from other island conferences are considered, the Moravian establishment in the region already looks like big business. The temptation to visualize bishops sitting back at general headquarters in Antigua, drooling as they count returns from churches spread around the region, Antigua(11), Barbados(10), St. Croix USVI & St. Thomas USVI(8), St. Kitts(4), Tobago(8) and Trinidad(5). Giving a combined church stock of forty-six churches, ignoring small churches, which are satellite organizations attached to larger ones. Assessment and billing of churches are set individually; not as island communities where superintendents are supposed to be in control. The bishops in Antigua, as far as the cash goes, want their money directly. Thus, from St. Kitts alone, each year they collect close to US$120,000.00. Assuming the same working average quota for the other church communities, gives an estimated US$1,380,000.00 per year income and that is controlled by the bishops. That is nearly one-and-a-half million United States dollars 'each and every' year that God sends! No wonder they are so greedy! Additionally, it is like trying to get blood out of stones when attempting to get them to spend money on church projects. Even salaries of individual field ministers that traditionally PEC are supposed to meet, an inherited responsibility, are reluctantly met. That attitude is detected from the number of times local priests complain to persons deemed capable of helping them out, about not being paid. Sometimes, claims of that type are suspected of being over-played. During any Synod year, host countries are responsible for taking care of resulting expenses. Like Synod, any extra activity, prescribed by PEC; the lucky country hosting it, gets to carry the cost of that extra project. Therefore, it is reasonable to have healthy doses of skepticism whenever PEC suggests that they spend money on projects. PEC provided salaries to field clergy are generally small compared to whatever the local salary rates are. Reasons being that ministers' living accommodations are provided, at no cost in any regard to them. Indeed, none of the household expenses that ordinary people have to pay are experienced by field ministers.

Their only routine expenditure is on food and even in that area; ministers have ways of organizing church members to provide aspects of meals for them regularly. The really, clever ones manage to get food requirements covered completely and so their greed is mainly to accumulate sizeable reserves in their bank accounts to take back home, probably for bragging purposes.

Earlier in this book, the dearth of compassion was one of the flaws pervading the Moravian mafia. Here too, in the area of church taxation and wealth collection, the same trait is evident. Below is an example, which blatantly shows how priority of field pastors appear to be programmed and the inflexibility embedded in that lack of compassion. – Shortly after the present, incumbent minister arrived at Zion Moravian church. He announced to attendants at a Sunday morning service gathering, "There is a message here from PEC. One of the churches here from this island community, has been in arrears with its quota payments for some time. The extent of the arrears originally amounted to over Seventy Thousand dollars. PEC informs that already it forgave that particular church community Forty Thousand dollars and it was not in the mood to forgive any more. In other words, that unidentified church still owes PEC over Thirty Thousand dollars and settlement of it is immediate. Furthermore, if the money owed plus the monthly quota commitment is not brought up to date by the time of the next Synod", which at that time was ten months away. He continued, "If the outstanding debt from that congregation is not made good in the time span of ten months, no seats at Synod will be available for the entire island conference." As far as PEC is concerned, the problem, which once belonged to a specific church transformed into one for the whole island Moravian community to deal with. Clearly, PEC suspected that the indebted church had financial problems and turned the commitment from the individual church into an island wide one. Furthermore, my analysis of the situation suggested that to comply with PEC's demand, the remainder of the island's combined churches, the other three and a bit churches, had to find an extra Ten Thousand dollars each month and for the next ten months if PEC was to be satisfied.

Such a requirement would have stretched the entire Moravian community of the island to unreasonable limits and most certainly would have been impossible. By any reasonable morale standard, the logic of the demand-twist was not only, unfair, it was also dishonest. When it suited the bishops, churches got individual treatment; because there was a problem, the determination to pump money out of the island changed the relationship and it became convenient to see and treat the island as one community, in order to get the money. That to my mind reflects the blatant greed of the Moravian clergy set of the region. The letter below suggested a logical solution with a view to fixing that situation amicably.

Before producing the letter however, the tone with which the new minister broke the news to the church could be revealing. Since he was not superintendent when the debt occurred, he wanted the problem cleared up quickly. Certainly, before he got his feet properly under the table of stewardship. He wanted to start with a clean slate as it were. However, 'come what may' that money was going to be paid was his clear intent, suggested by his attitude and the style in which he spoke. The huge obstacle was that the 'kitty' was empty; no money in it, on account that the overdraft situation was so bad that whenever cash went in, it disappeared into what effectively was a bottomless pit. Regardless of that, he was not going to take responsibility for am island conference that was on the bad financial side of PEC. Whatever had needed doing, he would see to it that the debt to PEC was resolved. The embedded unreasonableness of the situation did not occur to him nor did it register that the problem went beyond what it looked like on the surface and to perpetuate a bad situation was just plain stupid! At that point, the analytic capabilities of the author kicked-in with the letter below:

"Mr. Samuel Nathan,

New Road, St. Peters,

St. Kitts.

Tel.: 465 0742.

November 14, 2008.

The Chairman,

Board of Church Stewards,

Zion Moravian Church,

Mr. Chairman,

I write to comment and offer suggestions, triggered by the recently revealed debt, incurred over the past 'Four plus' years by short payments of imposed QUOTAS on some other Moravian (not Zion) church within the St Kitts family of churches.

That the above situation was allowed to get to the stage it has, could only have been the responsibility of the immediate past Superintendent on St. Kitts.

It would appear that the 'Eastern Moravian Province (Antigua) should have been told that the imposed Quota for the errant church here was unreasonable and could not be sustainably met, due to whatever the circumstances were and this would have been a function of the then Superintendent. However, since there was failure to perform properly in that regard; it seems to me, it is now the duty of the present incumbent to collate the necessary statistics, which would demonstrate and make the case to Antigua. Thereby, alerting PEC to the unreasonableness of the quota system that existed then and as far as I know, still prevails. To threaten this congregation and indeed, the entire St. Kitts, Moravian Community with the non-seating at Synod next, is unfair, unjust and diabolical! Especially since we are expected to pay somewhere in the region of XCD$500,000.00 for that Synod! This being the nominated, host country.

The perceived attitudes behind such an outrageous edict are indicative of the absurd church government system, employed by modern day Moravian hierarchy. A system, that clings desperately to pre-colonial principles. We live in democratic times but the Moravian system of government ignores standards that democracy demands, preferring to perpetuate arrangements that suit the bishops in Antigua; rather than administer clerical justice, reasonable treatment and consideration for justifiable concerns of congregations.

You the Chairman is supposed to be the elected representative for the Zion congregation. It is your function to run the church on behalf of members, including giving directions to the minister, who is supposed to be a servant of the church. What has evolved is an arrangement where the Chairman tends to be used as a 'rubber stamp' and minister's errand boy. That is unsatisfactory and is why the previous pastor has 'gone and left us' with an apparent bottomless overdraft-debt, because he was not, properly supervised. It is the Chairman's function to control all aspects of church business. Indeed, the collection of Chairmen within the St. Kitts Conference should oversee activities of the Superintendent! Failure to do so could result in more surprises every time they are changed!

P.s. I warned the church before about such an eventuality!!

S. Nathan.

Cc: sitting pastor & Church Notice Board."

As the intent of the circulation notice suggested, one copy of the above letter went to the minister on the Tuesday after the letter's date, another posted on the notice board inside the church, immediately before the next Sunday morning service. Ten minutes later, the minister removed it from the notice board, giving the impression that he was stalking the board, looking for that letter with the aim of removing it. The act of removing the notice board copy clearly indicated the level of intent to keep ordinary members out of touch with what goes on within the church's life. That action of the minister indicated his intention and suggests the underhand tactics he and others like him, are capable of using. That for me was a meaningful glance into their clandestine world and is cause for suspicion about other areas of church administration.

That there was no response to my letter reinforces suspicion about the intended secrecy. Although the letter's addressee was the Chairman, it is the minister, who controls the church and its functions, including those of the Chairman. That he tore the letter down from the church's notice board supports that view.

One suspected noticeable reaction to the letter was that two Sundays later, the minister took great pride in telling the church that in recent days a sum of XCD 2,800.00 dollars was sent to PEC as payment towards the standing debt. I wonder if anyone was impressed because really, that was just a 'drop in the ocean' and hardly went anywhere near the required solution of the real problem.

The reason for writing to the Chairman instead of the minister intended to make the point that, in my view, it should be the Chairman, who controls the church on behalf of the congregation. A competent Chairman who knew about life would never have allowed the church finances to deteriorate to the state it got to and still is. Alas, the history of elected officials within the church is most definitely one of the tools that ministers use to perpetuate their control over church life.

The system of electing officials to the two main church boards effectively works in a most skewed manner. The minister invites members from the congregation, requesting permission to use them as candidates for pending elections, which take place in each year, on the last Sunday of January at the annual church council meeting. He, the minister actually decides the board in which to place individual names. Lists of candidates appear for the first time during the annual church conference and members present invited to vote for the number of vacant seats needed for both boards, either the Board of Stewards or the Board of Elders.

The Elders are the group of members responsible for helping the minister with 'out-of-church' pastoral work: encouraging members, whose attendance lapsed, visiting sick, elderly or shut-in members and generally be available to assist the minister in his herding tasks.

The Board of Stewards are supposed to be the decision makers, the organization which directs and controls matters affecting church organization and direction. At least that is the theory of its function.

No elected member can sit on more than one board. The minister collates and announces successful elected officials at the end of the council meeting. Point to note: it is the minister who performs the original selections as to whom is put up for election to each board. The suggestion being that if for whatever reason, the pastor thinks that a particular individual is unsuitable by his criteria; that person never gets invited to stand for election to any of the boards, under his tenure. Unsuitable in this sense means any person who attracts the minister's disfavour, for whatever reason and especially if that individual has

ideas about proper management of the church, a stance that would inevitably put 'him or her', in conflict with objectives of the minister. Human nature being what it is, any minister with devious aims would seek to avoid having such a person on the supposedly management team of the church. Results of careful 'selections to boards' processes are that they generally end up with a bunch of individuals who do not know what they are about but take to themselves airs of importance and more disastrously, become a bunch of 'yes' men and women. With such groups, of course ministers get to please themselves in what they do or how they behave.

Probably the only directive from the 'Moravian Book of Order' observed by Zion is the rule, which stipulates that no member can serve continuously, for more than seven years on any board. After seven years, members who last that long without being bored, hardly agree to repeat the experience. All that is, except for the 'yo-yo' Chairman of Stewards, he is again in limbo, having just completed his second term as Chairman. The suspicion is that he is waiting out another year before qualifying to re-enter the Steward's team. That individual has a long, chequered professional, public and social profile. A one time public official of high rank, believed to be due to political nepotism, who at the time of writing, holds the position as Chairman of the other major political party, not in Government but trying.

To the intelligent observer, it is clear that our church has a latent political skew in favour of the national party of which the 'church's 'yo-yo' Chairman' also chairs. The out-of-church political status and loyalty carries over to inside church activities and so the dual Chairman enjoys that transcendent support. The Political status makes the 'yo-yo' Chairman, if not the most prominent 'lay member'; close to it. In terms of church welfare and overt dedication to interests of the congregation, he is sadly deficient.

There was a period during his Chairmanship when he got automatic respect as a consequence of his church status. It was a time shortly after the system of church government was discovered to be

colonialist in character. Quite a lot of time was spent, trying to convince the 'yo-yo' chairman that it was necessary to bring the Zion system of government in line with the national one, that is initiate steps to make church politics more democratic.

With hindsight, it looked like the minister and yo-yo chairman had agreements to manipulate the congregation for their own purposes. From the chairman's position, whenever any culturally religious activities went on in the church, the newspaper, labeled as the mouthpiece to the chairman's party, would send its cultural correspondent to cover the program and that reporter would swamp the centre pages with pictures from the event. No other church got such pervasive coverage from that newspaper for their cultural performances. The minister for his part received much praise and publicity in the process and was able to do pretty much as he pleased in other areas of church activity, without objections from the Chairman. It looked to be a lovely quid-pro-quo arrangement set between them. No amount of verbal arguments about the minister's performance or church administration had any influence on either of the top duo. Thus, it was necessary to take my concerns to the next annual conference. There I read the following comments, and then gave copies to select members:

"Church Comments

I have long resisted the urge to attend these meetings because of my tendency to get really, emotional at them.

However, events have got too confusing for me to remain silent; since this opportunity exists I use it to share with the church my thoughts. It is my sincere wish that these comments be given some consideration and I hope that the necessary adjustments in attitudes, conduct and practice might result:

It is time that my uncomfortable view about communications and other matters pertaining to this church are aired.

For a start, the rules that apply to the government of this church are woefully out of date, they belong to an age when monarchs dictated life for its subjects and to this day a degree of that expectation can be seen at work here at Zion. Leading to the view that you the minister is in complete control of all you survey, even to the point of over ruling those elected by our congregation. That is not how democratic organizations work. That sense of power no doubt, encourages you to make unacceptable utterances occasionally.

Christendom is well aware that the sermon is an important feature of the service, as an instrument, it is subject to much abuse radiating from pulpits the world over. Zion is no exception, which does not mean that it is any less pleasant when it happens. Silently, much offense are suffered when utterances suggesting that if what you say is not liked, then those displeased can stay away. Congregations of any dimension should not have to listen to that kind of talk from any pulpit. Remember that many of us were Moravians before you was even heard of and to come here and treat us as though we were backward children is in my view disrespectful. I do not see any member of this church, desirous of being spoken to like that. Nor, do we need to be used as 'sounding boards' about the implied relative positives of your native land; we Kittitians are proud of what we are and I personally feel that my country outstrips yours in every regard. Reference of that kind ought to be avoided at all times.

The information flows of this church, especially towards the 'grassroots' is an area worthy of some comment: seems that it is mainly items designed to generate finance that are thrown into the congregation. Reports related to irresponsible spending of church monies, bad judgment and greed are, almost never officially passed down. Suggesting, to my logic that a high degree of conspiracy of silence exists. The truth about silence designed to mislead or keep the congregation in ignorance is dishonesty and whatever form it is portrayed as, makes it inconsistent with biblical teachings. The hope here is that the contradiction is not lost.

Communications is the fuel that drives relationships and within this church system, it has been so badly slanted as to be considered encouragement for dishonest practices. Example: we get information functional to the running of Zion; when herding practices are judged to be desirable or the perpetual push to extract scarce resources from the congregation! What we do not get is full information indicating feedback about how extracted resources are expended, indicating absence of accountability and I am not talking about our situation here at Zion, since we can all see what is going on in our particular 'gold fish bowl.' Specifically: How the annual quote sent to bishops in Antigua is spent? There is a suspected aura that such matters are no concern of ours; yet we are significant contributors to the welfare of those who manage such resources. Why, a few years ago it was rumoured that those bishops were living like playboys; spending money like it was going out of fashion. It was also rumoured that plans for similar life style practices were to be imported here: you have your new vehicle around which, many untrue tales of its purchase were delivered from that very rostrum. It is also rumoured that you are in the enviable position to be one of the few clergies in receipt of child support allowance, yet the congregation have not to my knowledge been officially informed about that. These are things we should know rather than be left as subjects of guessing games. Can it be that if there were honest reporting about the way funds are spent; collections would suffer?

Greed in several guises is another of the bad virtues on display in this church. Lengthy examples could be used to illustrate that point but I will restrict myself in referring to the last sermon preached by the student priest: who diplomatically advised that God did not intend for earthly matters to take on such importance among those employed within the priesthood. To this day, I am of the view that the young student of the cloth was talking about what she observed in the manse connected to this church!

Can't help feeling that the evident bad practices evolved themselves into being, because, you have not properly been supervised by those elected to run this church. You appear to have it all your way, you travel out so frequently as to make ministers of government jealous, your in-church behaviour is poor, frequently walking around when you should be portraying an aura of clerical serenity from the rostrum.

Quite honestly, the perceived flaws in your performance are numerous and with concern for time, I will say finally that in reality, it is those elected to serve this congregation who are at fault for allowing you the minister to experiment with traditional Moravian ideals and taking advantage. Theirs, in particular the Chairman, are the responsibilities of seeing to it that this church, be properly served. They have allowed you to usurp the leadership that properly belongs to them and as a result, you have assumed almost absolute control of this church. Indeed, it is a ridiculously absurd situation. I do not know of any other working arrangement where an employee is paid to push around his employers. It is time that those elected by the church, perform to a better standard than presently exists, for only then will this air of confusion be lifted!

S. Nathan.

The original copy of the above was handed to the chairman, who sat next to the minister throughout the meeting. He accepted it with the comment, "Boy, Nathan had a lot to say here!" There was no comment from the pastor but no doubt, he got my meaning as did other members present, much to a great amount of embarrassment. Indeed days after that meeting, persons who were not present but know my outlook on church management accused me of being rude and abusive to the minister, some even invited me to find another church to attend. My interpretation of that reaction was the recognition of it being another manifestation of the sleepy attitude mentioned earlier.

No direct reply to the above contribution came from any sector of church management but I got an answer indirectly.

It came from the yo-yo chairman himself: two months after the council meeting and on the occasion of the minister's elevation. One of the big-shot bishops from Antigua performed the ceremony at Zion. My suspicion that the event had special orchestration got aroused but that was not my reason for not attending the affair. However, the Sunday morning service following the elevation ceremony, during the notice section, the chairman announced to us and the minister, "When the bishop performed the consecration service, he told this church to give the minister its full support. Therefore reverend, as far as I am concerned, this church is right behind you and where ever you lead we will follow!" He of course spoke for himself; certainly not for me!

I interpreted what the yo-yo chairman said as an abdication of his duties also the answer to my appeal for improved democratic practices within the church system of government and for the elected officials to be more prominent in their leadership roles. That remark by the chairman was like a slap in my face. Afterwards, I tried to remonstrate with the him about his attitude and was bluntly told, "You are wasting your time! What the bishop said is the way it is going to be and that is that!"

The after effects are: that minister has now left the church with a heavy in debt burden, an overdraft that is so deep, no one who knows the extent would talk about it. The replacement minister, on arrival moved into a hotel because he deemed that the manse was in an unacceptable state for habitation, exactly the same thing happened when his predecessor first moved into the manse three years earlier. Self same reason was that previous occupiers left the place in filthy conditions and I would not be too surprised if history repeats itself when the present incumbent leaves. Modern ministers are not very clean or hygienic people, seems they have not heard that 'Cleanliness is next to Godliness', If there is anything in that cliché, not many Moravian ministers are going to end up in heaven. They are too crocked anyway!

In recent months, it was discovered that the yo-yo chairman, who at the time of writing is serving one year in limbo as church chairman, the bet is that he will resume that role for a third time when his period of grace passes. However, let not your hearts be troubled for he now has a place on the provincial council. That is the PEC, which is the main 'rubber stamp' for the top body of Moravian churches of the East, Southeast and South Caribbean region. He has not been democratically elected, but appointed by the church regional big shots, the bishops, which prompts guesses as to what he had to do to get that? This author cannot help but wonder: what the price was? Did the yo-yo chairman sell-out the congregation and Zion for the price of that seat? It has been said that one requirement of politicians is that they lack consciences; the yo-yo chairman is a self-confessed politician, does his elevated seat debacle support that absent conscience principle?

In the mean time, Zion Moravian church and others directed by modern mafia type ministers around the region suffer bulldozing pressures towards evangelical practices at the expense of what used to be Moravianism. Caring members of the faith, who understand what is happening, do not like it but lack resources to react against that trend. Most of the shanghaied captive congregations do not even realize they are being, religiously hijacked and it is doubtful that they care, however, time will tell!

The latest word is there are signs that the promised imported decadent life style, enjoyed by bishops in Antigua, is most definitely in the planning stage here. The last council meeting enjoyed the news from the yo-yo chairman, who was not even active at the time but is at the stage of beginning to get confused with ownership. He told the meeting that the manse is unsuitable habitation for the new minister and the church (he) plans to buy a pastors residence in one of the 'up-market' areas, cost of XCD600,000.00 (US$225,000.00).

No one should be at all surprised, if it later emerges that the proposed new residence is really the idea of the incumbent minister, since he is the carrier of those decadent standards already prevalent in his and his colleagues, in Moravian mafia homeland.

Days after the council met, I was told, that when the yo-yo chairman broke news of the plan to the meeting, several members shouted in unison: "Where is Nathan? Why is he not here?" Don't know what they think I could have done about the news? Thank God, I was snugly comfortable at home where my blood pressure was kept nicely under control.

Quite honestly, they really should not worry for the church has no money, the sleepy congregation most certainly is not going to contribute sufficiently for that foolishness, no matter how many begging/taxing letters are sent to them and no sensible bank will lend money to an establishment that is already so deeply in debt.

I now attend another church where the serenity that I once felt after Moravian Sunday morning services, is gently returning! Especially, since I no longer have to perpetually survive, through those absurd, extended 'jump-up' sessions, whenever I go to worship God!

SUMMARY.

Reports that the real Sicilian brotherhood or Cosa Nostra is an organization that destroys 'human and related' entities and referred to generally, to as the Mafia. It is the reputed destructive qualities of that organization, with which the last word in the title of this book identifies. That is because of the destructive nature of the new Moravian ministry set, which is so pervasive within the church. The widespread nature of their devastating potential, perceived to be part of some plan, colluded to rather than individual spontaneity makes it feel like a devised arrangement. Indeed, when comparisons are made, barring accidents, the original Mafiosi destroys entities that are offensive or harmful to them, but this Moravian bunch, targets church organizations that have not done anything to them, have not molested or troubled them in any way. Those religious thugs just take it upon themselves to spiritually obliterate centuries old practices, recklessly annihilating established practices, obliterating long standing Moravian traditions and without batting an eyelid, replaced what was there with their personal agendas regardless of suffering caused, discomfort, inconvenience or damaging effects on indigenous needs of church and community, because they fancy replacing it with some other 'worship form' that is already widespread, regardless of the harm, distress and suffering caused to older and devoted followers of the faith. The young do not yet know anything better!

It may be that the word 'mafia' part of the title is too mild to describe the combined destructive attitude of that group. Alas, a term indicating their more horrific qualities is difficult to think of but I feel that 'mafia' will do nicely. The telling aspect of the apparent conspiracy is that it appears to be concentrated among ministers who hail from the seat of Moravian head quartered country. It was thought at one time that maybe, there was something in the Antiguan water motivating them to such ruthlessly diabolic behaviour, because non-Antiguan Moravian preachers do not exhibit the destructive tendencies as their Antiguan colleagues.

Analysis suggests that the rut towards the demise of the movement, which began centuries ago by men like John Wycliffe, Jan Hus, Martin Luther and Count Zinzendorf, men who sacrificed so much including lives, for the belief that would later evolve into the Moravian faith. The indications are, this is the era, when we are witnessing the beginning-of-the-end to the movement and it is just a question of time before the regional deathblow takes effect. Afterwards, buildings that used to house churches that previously conducted Moravian practices will continue being used for prayers and services. The unenlightened will keep calling them by names with Moravian as the first part, but really and truly, what will be happening inside of those establishments will not resemble anything, even close to what being Moravian was about, because this mafia set will have, between them, massacred the faith!

If the reader senses anger in my mood then the meaning will be properly passed on because I am angry! Furious, with those religious thugs, who robbed me of my Moravianism without 'by your leave', I am also angry with those fellow Moravians, who should know better but by their inaction, allowed those white ministerial collard destructors to regionally rob us of a dear and treasured style of worship. One, that once lost cannot be replicated and future generations will never know what it was like to be Moravians! In time to come, Moravian churches here will feel like any other evangelist or 'sideway church' and that will be a great loss because the Moravian ethos is one that allows members to worship with personal and spiritual independence. I sincerely hope and trust that international brothers of the faith continue to enjoy intact, Moravian or Lutheran practices and with unblemished 'IDEALS'.

MORAVIAN
MAFIA